PAUL
SIMON

PAUL SIMON

STILL CRAZY AFTER ALL THESE YEARS

PATRICK HUMPHRIES

D O U B L E D A Y

New York   London   Toronto   Sydney   Auckland

*B
SIMON*

Published by Doubleday, a division of Bantam
Doubleday Dell Publishing Group, Inc.
666 Fifth Avenue, New York, New York 10103

Doubleday and the portrayal of an anchor with
a dolphin are trademarks of Doubleday, a
division of Bantam Doubleday Dell Publishing
Group, Inc.

Library of Congress
Cataloging-in-Publication Data

Humphries, Patrick.
   [Boy in the bubble]
   Paul Simon, still crazy after all these years /
   Patrick Humphries.
   p.   cm.
   Originally published in Gt. Brit. under title:
The boy in the bubble.
   ISBN 0-385-24908-X:
   1. Simon, Paul, 1941–   .   2. Rock
musicians—United States—Biography.
I. Title.
ML420.S563H85   1989
784.5′0092′4—dc 19
[B]   88-30030
                                                     CIP

ISBN   0-385-24908-x
Copyright © 1988 by Patrick Humphries

First published in Great Britain in 1988
by Sidgwick & Jackson Limited

All Rights Reserved
First Edition in the United States of America
February 1989
BG

To Sue Parr, whose inspiration, support and collaboration helped me immeasurably in the completion of this book, and also for the past five happy years. Muse, typewriter repairer, word processor and all else. With all my love, and the promise that I will cut the grass this year . . .

To the memory of Eric Stanley Humphries, 'that silver haired Daddy of mine', 1920–86.

Contents

Acknowledgements

I would like to thank the following for their help, eternal vigilance and support. Their time, views and insights proved invaluable during the writing of this book:

Ian A. Anderson
Jane Armitage, for TCP
Kathy Began
Margot Bourlet
British Defence and Aid Fund
  for Southern Africa
Spencer Bright, for PG tips
Bill Brooke
Roy Carr
Chris Charlesworth
Dave Davies
Sue Foster
Pete Frame
Lon Goddard
Geoff Gough
Bob Harragan
Bruce Hawkins
Susan Hill
Peter K. Hogan
Peter Holt
Susie Howard
Mr P. Ish
Victoria Kingston
Jonny Kremer

Spencer Leigh, then and now
Dave Marsh
Hugh Masekela
Tony Molyneux
Sheila Parsons
D. A. Pennebaker
Roseinnes Phahle
Judith Piepe
Terri Robson
David and Jean Rugg
Rosalind Russell
Joseph Shabalala
Robert Shelton
Mark Smith
Chris Stern
Al Stewart
Liz Thomson
Chris Welch
John and Gael Whelan
Wally Whyton
Bob Woffinden
Ian Woodward
Richard and Claire Wootton

The Paul Simon Appreciation Society were of great help while I was writing this book. They scrupulously monitor every facet of

Paul Simon's career, and can be contacted at PO Box 32, Kendal, Cumbria, LA9 7RP, England.

The following publications are gratefully acknowledged for their articles, interviews and reviews used in this book:

Azania Frontline	*New Musical Express*
Billboard	*The Observer*
Crawdaddy	*Playboy*
Daily Telegraph	*Pulse*
Disc	*Q*
Folk Roots	*Record Collector*
The History of Rock	*Record Mirror*
Hot Press	*Rolling Stone*
The Independent	*Sounds*
Mail On Sunday	*Spin*
Melody Maker	*The Times*

Introduction

In the small Memphis suburb of Whitehaven stands one of rock music's most revered landmarks. Graceland, which appropriately enough had previously seen service as a church, was bought by Elvis Presley for $100,000 in 1957 while he was at the height of his powers, a sneering twenty-two-year-old who in two short years had cut a swathe through the cosy, middle-aged conformity of Eisenhower's America. Built in the early 1940s by a Dr Moore and named after his Aunt Grace, it was at Graceland that Elvis died tragically early in obese seclusion in August 1977, thus transforming the mansion for all time into a shrine. In the years following Presley's death millions have annually made the pilgrimage to Graceland. It has become a rock and roll Lourdes, the temporal and spiritual home of the King, a sanctuary for '*poorboys and Pilgrims*'. In 1982 Paul Simon and his young son Harper were among the visitors – like so many others of his generation, Simon felt that the impact of Elvis on his own life and music had been incalculable. It was thanks to Graceland, and all it stood for, that Simon felt he had '*a reason to believe/We all will be received in Graceland*'.

Abbey Road will be linked forever with the Beatles, Asbury Park with Springsteen, and Big Pink is inseparable from the Dylan mythology; even more than these, Graceland has always held a uniquely powerful place in rock iconography. In 1986, however, it came to mean more than just the empty shrine of the dead Elvis. Its very name and associations had been hijacked by Paul Simon to represent a sweeping new break in popular music. *Graceland* has now become the most controversial album of the 80s, a fact which Simon himself could hardly have foreseen as he followed the well-trodden track to the hallowed Memphis mansion.

Good Rockin' Tonight

In 1986 Paul Simon sang *'every generation throws a hero up the pop charts'*, and there is no doubt at all that the hero in the 1950s was Elvis Aron Presley. More than that, Elvis was the catalyst for the simmering mood of mid-50s' American youth; along with James Dean he virtually invented the teenager, and after Dean's untimely death in 1955, Elvis was left alone to rock the nation.

As a fifteen-year-old, Paul Simon couldn't help but get hooked into what was going on around him. The young Paul had two obsessions – baseball and rock and roll – which have stayed with him throughout his life. For Paul, Elvis was more than a temporary hero: he was the blueprint for all that followed. In 1980 Simon told Ray Coleman: 'The rock'n'roll solo performer was defined by Elvis Presley, the quintessential rock'n'roll star.' Simon grew his hair to emulate his idol, and once spent a day scouring New York for a lavender shirt just like Presley's. The Elvis fascination has stayed with Simon throughout his career, most overtly in his 1980 film *One Trick Pony*, which deals with growing old gracefully in rock and roll. But the ultimate homage to Elvis and the culmination of his influence on Paul's whole career occurred when Simon named his finest ever album *Graceland*.

The Elvis that Simon revered was the Elvis who mesmerized the world. Back in the stifling summer of 1954 in Memphis' Sun Studios, Elvis had almost single-handedly invented rock and roll, fusing white country and western with black rhythm and blues for the first time. His five Sun singles were no more than a regional event, but by the time he recorded his first sides for RCA in 1956, Elvis had become a national phenomenon. That year the world began to take notice.

'There was certainly something very mysterious for me, growing up in New York and hearing his music for the first time', Simon told Andy Peebles thirty years later. 'Even hearing his *name* for the

1

first time . . . almost like it was from another planet . . . when Presley appeared on the Tommy Dorsey or Ed Sullivan shows, it was a gigantic cultural earthquake.'

The young Simon, however, was musically eclectic, revelling also in the doo-wop groups which proliferated around New York in the mid-50s – the Penguins, the Moonglows, the Orioles, the Five Satins are chanted like a litany on 1983's 'René and Georgette Magritte With Their Dog After The War' from the *Hearts & Bones* album. Simon also liked the near-acapella sounds of groups like the Monotones, the El Dorados and the Cadillacs, and these naturally led him on to discover gospel, including Sam Cooke when he was with the Soul Stirrers, and the Swan Silvertones, who represented a rich and varied strand of popular music which Simon would eventually use creatively in his own music.

For Paul Simon, as for other youngsters in the mid-50s, the chief opportunity for hearing these new and invigorating types of music was courtesy of Alan Freed's radio show *Moondog Rock'n'Roll Party*. Freed was the legendary DJ who first popularized the phrase 'rock and roll', and his Moondog show was required listening for a whole generation of fledgling rock idols – the Band even named their 1973 album of cover versions, *Moondog Matinee*, after Freed's massively influential show. Like the young John Lennon, 3,000 miles away in Liverpool with his ear glued to Radio Luxembourg, the only European outlet for the new rock and roll, Paul Simon was fascinated by the sounds pouring from Freed's WINS show, and prepared himself for the next big step for a rock and roll-obsessed teenager, the switch from listening to others' music to making his own.

The impact of rock and roll on 1950s' America is not hard to understand. Eisenhower was half-way through a term which epitomized complacency and dull, traditional values. Senator Joe McCarthy was rampaging against Reds under the bed, and the Cold War was at its height. Although Marlon Brando and James Dean had just invented method acting, the traditional values of old Hollywood still held sway. However the crewcut conformity was about to be shattered once and for all. The dissatisfied youth focussed on Jack Kerouac's haphazard Beat odysseys and the gyrating pelvis of Elvis Presley. Elvis blitzkrieged the nation; the mopping up was done by classic rock and rollers like Jerry Lee Lewis, Little Richard, Buddy Holly, Eddie Cochran and Gene Vincent. Then there were the one-offs, the one-hit wonders, the mavericks the music industry would chew up and spit out, like

Johnny Ace, Warren Smith, Buddy Knox – sad, solitary signposts on the road to other people's rock and roll glory.

Rock and roll in the 50s was primarily a youth cult, but its lasting importance lay in the seismographic impact it had on the middle class and the middle-aged. It also paved the way for the next generation of rock idols: while Elvis conveyed mystery, dark power and purpose, Paul Simon, John Lennon, Bob Dylan, John Fogerty, Bruce Springsteen and thousands more Elvis disciples sat awestruck, aware that this strange, unsettling sound would some-how, irrevocably be linked with their destinies.

Music had always played a large part in the Simon household. Paul's mother, Belle, was a teacher before her two children were born, and his father, Louis, was a stand-up bass player who performed regularly with orchestras on the Arthur Godfrey and Jackie Gleason TV shows. Paul later referred to this 'family bassman' in his 1970 song 'Baby Driver'. Paul's family encouraged him in his musical interests even as a very young child. Long before hearing Presley, Simon recalls singing along to a record of *Alice In Wonderland*, and his father's very serious comment, 'That's nice Paul – you have a nice voice.' This encouraged the young Paul, who determinedly carried on practising in the acoustic isolation of the family bathroom, fascinated by the echoing possibilities when hearing his voice rebound. His first guitar was bought for him by his parents on the occasion of his fourteenth birthday – it had cost them twenty-five dollars, and Paul devoted all his attention to learning how to play it, often practising with his brother, Eddie who, despite being four years his junior, shared Paul's love of music and baseball.

Paul Frederic Simon was born on 13th October, 1941 in Newark, New Jersey, but the family moved soon afterwards to the comfortable suburb of Forest Hills, where Arthur Garfunkel was born on 5th November, in the same year. The Simons enjoyed a contented middle-class existence in the borough of Queens. Their house was situated on 70th Road in Kew Garden Hills, only three blocks away from the Garfunkels' home. The two boys first met at a local school, PS164, where they appeared together in a production of *Alice In Wonderland*, with Paul as the White Rabbit and Art as the Cheshire Cat.

Simon recalls hearing a nine-year-old Garfunkel singing the aptly titled 'They Tried To Tell Us We're Too Young' at school and, impressed by Garfunkel's sway over an impressionable audience

3

of girls, Simon himself then sang for the first time in public. He remembers trying himself out on 'Anywhere I Wander', and soon he and Art were in a street corner doo-wop group called the Sparks. By their early teens the two were confident performers, and inspired by a duo from the Bronx called Robert and Johnny and their one-off hit 'We Belong Together', Simon became fascinated by the harmonic possibilities of a singing duo. Simon and Garfunkel began performing together at school concerts and local dances. Simon enjoyed creating harmonies, and he arranged an acapella version of the Crew Cuts' 'Sh-Boom' for one school concert, in which their fourteen-year-old voices were already weaving and blending together as one. They even tried their hand at writing songs together, copyrighting their first effort, called 'The Girl For Me', at the Library of Congress in 1955. Simon's parents continued to encourage their eldest son's musical activities, but, like other parents of the time, only so long as they didn't interfere with his school work.

Paul and Art's role models were the Everly Brothers, who broke nationally with 'Bye Bye Love' in May 1957, following it with their first Number 1, 'Wake Up Little Susie', later that year. Like Chuck Berry and Buddy Holly, many of the Everlys' best songs of the 50s were classic teen anthems; they were frequently written by Felice and Boudleaux Bryant, who presciently identified the 'abstract third' of the Everlys' harmonies, which would later become a hallmark of Simon and Garfunkel's work together. The Everlys' appeal was largely in the rock field, but they were adept at and drew inspiration from many different styles. Their authentic country and western background is unmistakable, as in 1958's *Songs Our Daddy Taught Us* and 1968's *Roots*, and it was from established country and western acts like the York Brothers and the Delmore Brothers that they took their harmonic lead. For Simon and Garfunkel, though, the most important appeal of the Everlys lay in their beguiling vocal harmonies, two voices more than doubling the emotional impact of one. Always proud of their rock and roll heritage, Simon and Garfunkel would, in later years, feature the Everlys' version of Gene Autry's sentimental 'That Silver-Haired Daddy Of Mine' in concert, and subsequently recorded 'Bye Bye Love' and 'Wake Up Little Susie'.

For the young Simon the appeal of working with Garfunkel was obvious: blessed with a voice of angelic purity, Garfunkel had swiftly acquired a reputation as the best singer in the neighbourhood. Simon remembers the impact of Art's early performances: 'Everyone, particularly girls, was very impressed with his singing . . . and I was very impressed that *they* were very impressed'.

Art's parents had two tape recorders, and weekends would often find the teenage Simon and Garfunkel experimenting with the machines looped up, recording their nascent harmonies, double-tracking and laying down tracks which, despite all their obviously home-grown elements, began to sound quite professional. Recognizing the manifold possibilities of working together, both boys became committed to making it as a duo. Garfunkel, a mathematics boffin and student of architecture, applied his cool logic to notating the pop charts in graph form, while Simon practised hard on the guitar and slowly developed his own songwriting style.

If you were young, white and a rock and roll songwriter in New York City in the 1950s, your Mecca lay at 1619 Broadway – the Brill Building (where, appropriately, Simon today has his office). It was here that the very best pop writers of the late 50s and early 60s clocked in and worked production-line style, supervised by the avuncular but businesslike Don Kirshner and his partner Al Nevins. Like Hollywood in its golden age, the Brill Building was a centre of excellence to which the very best were drawn. The Brill became home for writers like Neil Diamond, Barry Mann and Cynthia Weil, Neil Sedaka, Gerry Goffin and Carole King, Jerry Leiber and Mike Stoller. Barry Mann (who put the Bomp . . .) recalled the situation: 'It was insane. Cynthia and I would be in this tiny cubicle, about the size of a closet, with just a piano and a chair, no window or anything. We'd go in every morning and write songs all day.' Amazingly, those uninspiring closets produced many excellent songs, including such gems as 'Will You Love Me Tomorrow', 'It Might As Well Rain Until September', 'Then He Kissed Me', 'You've Lost That Lovin' Feeling', 'Oh Carol', 'Happy Birthday Sweet Sixteen' and many more.

It was into this competitive vortex that Simon and Garfunkel plunged themselves. Together they wrote songs in every spare moment, and would journey by the crosstown bus and subway into Manhattan, to the heart of the monster, the Brill Building itself. Once there, the two teenagers would wander round the warren of offices trying to interest publishers in their songs. The likelihood of two teenagers being taken seriously by hard-edged businessmen these days is remote, but in the heady innocence of the 1950s that's how stars were born. The fourteen-year-old Frankie Lymon was a

5

big star at the time. Such was the insatiable demand for rock stars, however, that, discovered at thirteen, he was a has-been by fifteen.

Together, Paul and Artie were developing into effective hustlers who refused to be downcast by the number of doors slammed in their faces. By this time they already had a couple of years' experience, and time was still on their side, but with the usual impatience of youth they were desperate to make it big, and quick. Garfunkel found the experience of selling their songs intimidating, but admired Simon's resolution. Simon remembers each audition as being pretty much the same for the two tenacious teenagers: 'There'd be a secretary in a two-room office, and we'd say, "We write songs and sing". I'd take out my $25 guitar and we'd just stand up and sing. I think we even signed a recording contract when we were fourteen.'

The big break eventually came after a long slog. One song the boys had written together and tried out at school dances had been particularly well received, so they decided to risk recording a cheap demo of it. One afternoon at a local studio Simon and Garfunkel cut 'Hey Schoolgirl'; hanging round the studio with one of his acts waiting for the next available studio slot was a song-plugger called Sid Prosen, who overheard the song and informed the teenagers in the time-honoured showbiz tradition that they were 'the greatest thing since the Everly Brothers. I'm going to make stars out of you!'

By 1957 rock and roll was changing. The initial explosion had been replaced by a smoother, silkier sound; even Elvis' anarchy had been harnessed, and he was releasing songs like 'Too Much' and 'All Shook Up'. Meanwhile, the cleaner, more acceptable face of white rock and roll was that of Pat Boone, who had three Number 1s that year: the slushy 'Don't Forbid Me', 'Love Letters In The Sand' and 'April Love'. Other Number 1 hits of 1957 included Tab Hunter's schmaltzy 'Young Love', Debbie Reynolds' 'Tammy', Johnny Mathis' 'Chances Are', and Perry Como's 'Round And Round'. Rays of hope, though, came courtesy of Sam Cooke, the Crickets and the Everly Brothers, who hit the top spot before the year was out.

Obviously the tiny, dark Simon and tall, blonde Garfunkel couldn't be realistically marketed as brothers, and in the ethnically anxious days of 1957 they certainly wouldn't have stood a chance if they had called themselves Simon and Garfunkel. A pseudonym was required fast, and so the two sixteen-year-olds became Tom and Jerry. Paul Simon was now professionally known as Jerry Landis (he was dating a girl called Sue Landis at the time), while Arthur Garfunkel became Tom Graph, after the way he whiled away his time plotting the courses of all the hit records on big sheets of graph paper. Re-christening complete, Tom and Jerry's 'Hey Schoolgirl' was quickly pushed into the rock and roll arena on the Big label, and to everyone's delight it became a hit!

The single hung around the *Billboard* Hot 100 for over two months, peaking at Number 54 and selling 100,000 copies. The royalty rate for such success ensured that Simon could buy his first car, a red Impala convertible, which soon met a flaming end when its carburettor burnt out near Garfunkel's house. Simon wistfully recalled: 'I ended up watching while my whole share of the record burned up!' To ensure that Tom and Jerry's fifteen minutes of fame were exploited to the full, the duo were hustled off on a package tour, which was headlined by LaVern Baker and bolstered by Little Joe and the Thrillers. 'We were the token white act,' remembered Garfunkel.

The real high point of Tom and Jerry's career was their appearance on the massively popular *American Bandstand* TV show on 22nd November, 1957. Topping the bill was the Killer – Jerry Lee Lewis – pounding through his new release, a little number called 'Great Balls Of Fire'. Simon admitted that Jerry Lee was a hard act to follow with their matching red jackets and crew cuts. Nevertheless, it was a heady experience for the two boys. Only the month before they had been diligently watching Dick Clark on *Bandstand*, and now, four weeks later, they were guests on the same show, a situation which certainly did no harm to their standing at school and in the neighbourhood. 'You can't imagine,' Simon recalled years later, 'what it was like having a hit record behind you at the age of sixteen. . . . It was an incredible thing to have happen to you in your adolescence. I had picked up the guitar because I wanted to be like Elvis Presley – and there I was!'

The history of rock and roll, however, is peppered with one-hit wonders, a lost legion that Tom and Jerry were soon to join as their three subsequent singles 'Dancin' Wild', 'Our Song' and 'That's My Story' stiffed. Chastened, Tom and Jerry went back to school. During their brief career, though, they did manage to cut an album, produced by the pushy Mr Prosen. *Tom & Jerry* wasn't released in Britain at the time, and when it did come out on the Pickwick label in 1967 to cash in on the duo's success as Simon and Garfunkel, it had a misleadingly recent cover photograph of Garfunkel carrying a copy of A. J. P. Taylor's *History Of The First World War* (hardly required Tom and Jerry reading!); Simon and Garfunkel sued Pickwick, who soon deleted the album.

Listening to the album now, thirty years on, is a strange experience: on one level it epitomizes the anodyne state of rock and roll after Elvis' fusillade had faded and before the Beatles brought it all back home; but on another level it is fascinating to hear the vinyl debut of a duo whose best-known work came to represent the apogee of studio attainment and whose lyrics came to encapsulate the hopes, dreams, despair and aspirations of a whole generation. It is difficult to believe it is Paul Simon who sings here of such intense teenage experiences as, '*The teacher is lookin' over so I got to whisper way down low/To say wo bop a loo chi bop wo wo wo*'. The album is obviously heavily influenced by the Everly Brothers, with the embryonic Simon and Garfunkel harmonies tested out on such syrupy ballads as 'That's My Story' and the intense 'Teenage Fool', on which Simon also experiments with Elvis-style swoop and drop delivery. Two instrumentals credited to Simon/Prosen serve to pad out the album: 'Tia-juana Blues' and 'Simon Says' are both instantly forgettable cocktail bar muzak, surely only included to stretch the album to an acceptable five tracks a side. The eight vocal tracks all deal with the themes that filled the 50s' airwaves – teenage love (that's for *real*), juke boxes, high school hops, all the familiar ingredients of adolescent angst; a furrow which had already been ploughed more creatively by Chuck Berry, Eddie Cochran and Buddy Holly.

In later years, when he acknowledged them at all, Simon was particularly scathing about his Tom and Jerry years. In 1966 he told *Record Mirror* that his music nine years before was 'fodder for mental eunuchs . . . I'm ashamed of it. Fortunately we made it under another name. I thought that having a pop hit was great status, I wanted to be adored by everybody. By the age of nineteen I was very depressed, I thought I was over the hill, washed up already. I'd peaked at fifteen!' Simon's resentment was perhaps understandable: it was at a time when he was being pushed as the legitimate voice of folk protest, the thinking man's pop star, and he thought the audience who related to the angry, articulate 'Sounds Of Silence' would find it hard to reconcile that image with the sentiments of 'Dancin' Fool'.

Robert Shelton remembers interviewing Simon for a *New York Times* profile in 1966, and that Simon made no mention whatsoever of his Tom and Jerry period. Shelton recalls: 'I interviewed them both together in, I guess, what was their manager's apartment in the East

50s or 60s. I didn't do much probing, and there was not a clue about Tom and Jerry. . . . You see, they didn't want to jar their image in the folk world. . . . And foolishly, by wanting to conceal it, when the revelation came it rebounded back on them. . . . They were later very embarrassed by the release of the Tom and Jerry album. They tried to get it stopped, their lawyers were saying things like, "They had a unique identity in the popular music world and this destroyed it!" ' By 1970, Simon had mellowed sufficiently to admit to *Record Mirror*: 'If they'd released it saying, "This is Simon and Garfunkel at fifteen" it might have been interesting and I would have said, "Okay, that's me at fifteen and I'm not ashamed of it". I made a record at fifteen, and everybody wanted to at that age. I just wanted to be Frankie Lymon again.'

Tom and Jerry's album was actually no worse than those of their contemporaries, but it made no real impact at the time. However, with 'Hey Schoolgirl' the teenagers had tasted success and enjoyed it; the desperation to do so had now been assuaged, but they still continued to see music as a part of their joint future. The comfortable backgrounds of Paul Simon and Art Garfunkel and their stable, supportive families ensured that they didn't meet the same sad end as that other burnt-out teenage star of the era, Frankie Lymon, dead from a heroin overdose at twenty-five; while their relative lack of success meant that they didn't have to undertake the succession of rigorous package tours which claimed the lives of young hopefuls like Buddy Holly and Ritchie Valens. For many black kids in acapella street corner groups around New York City in the 1950s, rock and roll was a desperate gamble, a lifeline like basketball and boxing, which could, with luck, help them escape the ghettos. For them, music was the way out; for Tom and Jerry it was a successful hobby which they hoped would one day become a lucrative career. But that was all in the future, for by 1958 Tom and Jerry were again simply the names of cat and mouse cartoon characters. For his efforts as a teenage pop star, Paul Simon had acquired and lost his red Impala and an electric guitar. He'd made it to *American Bandstand*. He was seventeen years old and it was time to come down to earth.

The Lone Teen-Ranger

The world outside the Brill Building was bubbling along; by 1958 Eisenhower still had two years of his presidency to run, and no one was quite sure how his opposite number, Premier Khrushchev, would shape up in his first year of leadership. In Britain, wily old Harold Macmillan kept telling the electorate they'd never had it so good, which everyone swallowed, except Bertrand Russell who launched the Campaign for Nuclear Disarmament that year. The Cold War was on the back burner, Senator Joe McCarthy having died in ignominy in 1957, and teenage Americans were busy getting wrapped up in the hula-hoop craze, while other novelties like Sheb Woolley's 'Purple People Eater' and David Seville's 'Witch Doctor' topped the charts. In South Africa, though, there was little to smile about: the National Government was re-elected with an increased majority, which saw a strengthening of the already draconian apartheid laws.

The rock and roll fervour which bombarded the mid-50s had, by 1958, been emasculated. Little Richard enrolled at Bible college, while Elvis was inducted into the Army; Jerry Lee Lewis was hounded out of Britain after it was revealed that his new bride was his fourteen-year-old cousin, and *Billboard* began the probe into rock and roll payola which would eventually bring down Alan Freed. In New York Buddy Holly commenced what proved to be his last studio sessions, the fruits of which signalled a drift away from hard rock to ballads.

Art Garfunkel was thinking about a sensible career. He had enjoyed the Tom and Jerry experience, but considered it little more than a teenage aberration, and so he took himself off to Columbia University to study mathematics, while Simon opted for an English literature course at Queens College. The complexities of literature exuded a rich fascination, but Simon had been bitten by the rock and roll bug, and showed no sign of shaking off the symptoms. He somehow felt sure that his future lay in the colourful firmament of music rather than the fusty confines of academia.

The 'Hey Schoolgirl' experience had ensured that Paul Simon's (or rather Jerry Landis') name was well known to record executives, song pluggers and studio personnel around New York; and Simon got into the habit of leaving his name with companies or individuals who wanted to make quick twenty-five dollar demos to present to up-and-coming stars like Dion, Fabian and Bobby Vee. This workmanlike experience of recording studios in the late 50s proved to be an invaluable addition to his already established songwriting and guitar-playing abilities. Simon became a master of the recording process: double-tracking, overdubbing, using himself as *a poet and a one-man band*. He refined his microphone technique and developed other essential studio skills which were invaluable during the creation of the Simon and Garfunkel sound less than six years later.

Coincidentally, a fellow student of Simon's at Queens was one Carole Klein, later to achieve fame in her own right with her multi-million selling 1971 album *Tapestry*, when she was rather better known as Carole King. Carole was an exact contemporary of Simon and at fourteen had already formed her first group, the Cosines. In their late teens she and Simon sometimes worked together demoing songs for acts like the Fleetwoods and the Passions. Carole would play piano and drums, while Paul would concentrate on guitar and bass; then they would harmonize over the results. The most successful song from this partnership was 'Just To Be With You', which was a minor American hit for the Passions.

Despite the magnetism of music, Simon was conscious that a good education also had its place in his future. When Carole was keen to quit college and devote all her energies to rock and roll, Simon was emphatic in his advice: ' "Don't! You'll ruin your career." She quit, and had ten hits that year!' Later that same year, Carole King met and married her co-writer, Gerry Goffin, and the pair soon moved into the 'songwriting prison' of the Brill Building.

It is fascinating, if futile, to speculate just how different Paul Simon's career might have been had he followed Carole King into the Brill hit factory. But although Simon chose another route and indeed became a pioneer of the singer–songwriter trail, his later music retained many of the pop sensibilities and structures which were prevalent during the era when rock and roll coalesced into pop in the late 50s and early 60s. Like Chuck Berry, who in 'Maybelline' sings of the girl *'campaign shouting like a Southern diplomat'*, Simon's great talent is his acute eye for detail. Jerry Leiber and Mike Stoller also had that precision – one can imagine Paul Simon relishing lines like: *'The way we waltzed around those marble floors/You sure did look deluxe/In your white tie and tux/Up in that big white house that is no longer yours'* ('Don Juan'), or *'She had a picture of a cowboy tattooed on her spine/Saying Phoenix, Arizona 1949'* ('Little Egypt'). But Simon's apprenticeship was over, and as a craftsman in his own right he was about to become one of the handful of artists whose talents would break open the Tin Pan Alley/Brill Building stranglehold of popular music forever.

By the early 1960s, when Paul Simon began recording again under a bewildering array of pseudonyms, the pop scene was in a period of transition which would pave the way for the global knockout of the Beatles. Buddy Holly had been killed in an air crash in 1959, Eddie Cochran died in 1960 in the car crash that also left Gene Vincent badly injured, Elvis emerged from the Army in 1960 crooning 'Wooden Heart', the threat that rock and roll posed now eviscerated. Their replacements were manufactured teen idols like Fabian, Tommy Rydell, Bobby Vinton, all of whom were given generous slices of *American Bandstand* to promote the clean, keen images which found favour with parents, but which, as everyone from Elvis Presley to the Beastie Boys has found, will never do for the kids! While Buddy Holly, Chuck Berry and Eddie Cochran had written much of their own best material, none of the new breed did, so there was a massive demand for good new material. It was into that avaricious vacuum that Paul Simon now plunged.

Retaining his Jerry Landis pseudonym, Simon cut a number of one-off singles, only one of which – the engagingly titled 'Lone Teen-Ranger' – scraped into the Hot 100. 'Teen-Ranger' was a cute novelty cut, with plenty of sound effects; released in 1962 it was as amusing a one-off as pop has thrown up, the singer bemoaning the fact that his girlfriend prefers a fictional TV character to him. He also recorded 'Anna Belle' for MGM in 1959, and 'Play Me A Sad Song' in 1962. The latter is a classic teen ballad which finds Simon all alone on a Saturday night, pleading with the DJ to play him a sad song to match his mood, and is interesting for its foretaste of the isolation of 'I Am a Rock' four years later. Other Jerry Landis efforts included 'Shy', the fetching 'Flame', and the mildly provocative 'I'd Like To Be The Lipstick On Your Lips'. They were

12

all average pop fodder of the period, and few would have mourned Jerry Landis' passing.

Simon was also recording intermittently as Tico and The Triumphs, whose finest vinyl moment was the 1961 single 'Motorcycle', an effort which remains as good as any tribute to automania, from the Beach Boys through Chuck Berry to Bruce Springsteen; although not quite as memorable as the Cheers' 1955 cracker 'Black Denim Trousers And Motorcycle Boots', which was such a good song that even Edith Piaf was impelled to record it. Tico's other memorable contribution to teenage culture was the 1962 single 'Get Up And Do The Wobble'. Rush-released to cash in on Chubby Checker's Twist sensation, it was one of dozens of singles which tried to turn a largely disinterested audience onto dance crazes such as the Hucklebuck, the Slime, the Slop and the Mashed Potato!

While churning out unsuccessful singles under the guise of Jerry Landis and Tico, Simon was also busy working for a music publisher, plugging his own songs and producing and arranging sessions for other people. With such a diversity of activities it is hard to be sure, but Simon is rumoured to have produced songs for, amongst others, the Central High School Caf Band, Jay Walker and the Pedestrians, and Dougie and the Dudes. Another Simon involvement was with the Brooklyn based group, the Mystics, who enjoyed a Top 20 hit with 'Hushabye' in 1959. Simon wrote and arranged a slushy version of the traditional Welsh hymn 'All Through The Night' for them, and also sang lead on their 'Don't Tell The Stars' for a flat fee of $100.

Quite how Simon's English teachers at Queens reacted to such deathless works as 'The Wobble' and 'Lone Teen-Ranger' goes unrecorded, but however frivolous these activities seem in hindsight, they gave Simon more practice at writing to order and helped the mechanics of using a recording studio to become second nature to him. Perhaps even more invaluable, though, was the comprehensive understanding he gained of the financial and business sides of the music industry. Years later Simon recalled in an interview with Andy Peebles: 'I remember having a conversation with John Lennon and he said, "How did you know about these business moves?" Because the Beatles in the early days just signed away everything. I said, "Well we grew up in New York, we were around the music business and of course were cheated all the time." But at that age we didn't care and we had the pleasure of recording . . . our parents didn't strenuously discourage us . . . it wasn't a question of signing a record contract and quitting school or anything like that.'

On finishing university, Paul Simon left behind the world of recording studios, at his mother's behest, to study at law school. Judith Piepe, a London social worker who became friendly with Simon over the next few years, told me in 1982: 'Paul's mother wanted him to be a lawyer or a doctor, and it's the old story that if you can't stand the sight of blood, you become a lawyer! . . . His mother told him, "Music's all very well Paul, but you can't make a living out of it!" Famous last words!'

Simon spent six 'miserable' months studying law to keep his parents happy, but his heart was not in the dry legal language. Although at this time pop music in America had reached an impasse, there was a tremendous resurgence of interest in folk music, and by 1962/3 the folk sound was percolating out of every coffee house in Greenwich Village. The burgeoning interest in folk coincided with the growing civil rights movement and a general politicization of American youth, now freed from the witch-hunts of the McCarthy years. That growing awareness was linked to the bright young presidency of John F. Kennedy, elected in 1960, who had put civil rights high on his list of priorities. Eloquent spokesman for the disillusioned blacks was the charismatic, dynamic figure of Martin Luther King, who had first come to prominence as a twenty-six-year-old clergyman during the negro boycott of buses in Montgomery, Alabama in 1955, and had built up a devoted following across the USA in the intervening years.

It was the Kingston Trio's 1958 Number 1 hit, 'Tom Dooley', which first suggested that 'folk' music could be commercially acceptable, a position consolidated in 1962/3 by the success of Peter, Paul and Mary, which was largely due to them promoting the thought-provoking songs of Bob Dylan. Those with an interest in folk gravitated towards New York's Greenwich Village. In the city's Greystone Hospital, the venerated Woody Guthrie, titular head of the revival, lay dying, eaten up by Huntington's Chorea as he watched the new generation headed by Dylan, with the likes of Phil Ochs, Tom Paxton, Richard Farina, David Blue and Ric Von Schmidt in trail. By the time Paul Simon came to write his first 'serious' song, the folk revival was in full swing. As Dave Laing wrote in *The Electric Muse* in 1975 of the folk revival: 'Its strength and growth in the early 60s was based on its relevance to the set of social changes which were slowly beginning to work themselves out in America, and also on the particularly parlous state of pop music at that time. In a sense, the power of the revival was the result of the unlikely coincidence of Martin Luther King and Frankie Avalon!'

Simon couldn't help but be aware of the seismographic changes sweeping the country, and how the music he grew up with had failed to reflect those changes: 'Rock and roll got very bad in the early 60s, very mushy', he recalled in 1971. 'I used to go down to Washington Square on Sundays and listen to people playing folk songs . . . I liked that a whole lot better than Bobby Vee.' Like many others of his generation, Simon was knocked out by the purity of voice and intention of Joan Baez, who had blown the crowd away at the first Newport Folk Festival in 1959. Along with Peter, Paul and Mary, Baez was an early champion of Bob Dylan's pioneering work. It was largely thanks to Dylan that Simon came to appreciate that a song could express complex social issues concisely and effectively, that music had the potential to provoke a commitment which moribund forms such as the novel or film were no longer doing. For an articulate, politically aware youth such as Paul Simon, the appeal was obvious.

Dylan had previously released a patchy debut album but, following a formative trip to Britain in 1962, he unleashed the seminal *Freewheelin'* early in 1963. It contained both the anthemic 'Blowin' In The Wind' and the apocalyptic 'A Hard Rain's A-Gonna Fall'. It was Dylan who, almost at a stroke, gave pop music a voice, who single-handedly wrenched it away from the empty singing faces and gave it a poetry which the Beatles would then popularize – nothing would ever be quite the same again. In a 1968 radio interview, Simon conceded that before Dylan 'nobody was writing the truth. . . . He made it possible for the "Sounds Of Silence" to be a hit. He made it possible for a whole group of lyricists to come onto the scene. I just think we wouldn't be there if it wasn't for Dylan.' Even so, the inevitable comparisons to Dylan rankled with Simon, but Dylan had already become the yardstick by which other songwriters were measured, so all-embracing was his impact. From the bohemian kingdom of Greenwich Village, Dylan reigned supreme; the Village's citadel was Gerde's Folk City, situated on West 4th Street. Both Paul Simon and Art Garfunkel were regular visitors to Gerde's, which acted as a showcase for all the aspiring Dylans. Not unkindly, Gerde's was christened 'the Brill Building of folk music', and it was there on 30th March, 1964 that Paul and Art made their New York debut as Simon and Garfunkel.

Louie Bass was doorman and occasional waiter at Gerde's for two decades, and recalled Simon and Garfunkel's debut: 'I remember Simon and Garfunkel performing "The Sounds of Silence" for the first time at Folk City. They sang it at some sort of college reunion. At that time I never thought they would make it. They didn't sound as good as some of the other acts. It was the first time they tested it out publicly. They went over well because it was their friends.' Other Gerde's regulars recalled Simon and Garfunkel playing to a handful of disinterested customers who were surprised at their conservative image; the Gerde's crowds were pretty boisterous, and Simon would become visibly flustered at the lack of response his thought-provoking songs aroused.

Robert Shelton was folk music editor of *The New York Times* in the early 60s, and was a crucial figure in the development of the folk renaissance in New York, that city's inimical response to the 'British Invasion' of 1964. It was Shelton who first recognized Dylan's nascent talent, and his *New York Times* column kept readers informed of the best and the brightest new names on the scene. He remembered the period when I interviewed him in 1982: 'I think Simon was more influenced by the folk scene in Britain than the Greenwich Village folk scene. . . . He was in touch with some of the people, but he certainly wasn't a Village cat. . . . Simon and Artie were uptown guys, Queens guys. . . . I was struck by a kind of Mickey Mouse, timid, contrived side. And of course through Dylan, Van Ronk, all those guys, what was really being venerated was . . . a rough, ethnic, natural, dirty sound. They were sounding very suburban. He always struck me as a suburban type of Dylan.'

Simon was disenchanted with the response to his new work, and his own feelings were in tune with those of the nation. Following Kennedy's assassination in November 1963, the mood had changed. The nation plunged into prolonged and heartfelt mourning at the death of its favourite and fortunate son. The Camelot of his presidency had lost its Arthur, and was now ruled by Modred, in the shape of President Lyndon Johnson. Simon's generation took Kennedy's murder bitterly to heart. The negative mood permeated the nation, and only Europe seemed to offer some sort of hope. With the raging rise of Beatlemania, London was in the process of 'swinging'. As Philip Larkin wrote in his poem 'Annus Mirabilis': 'Life was never better than in nineteen sixty three. . . . Between the end of the Chatterley ban/And the Beatles first LP'.

As that Golden Age kaleidoscoped into 1964, the world's press sourly noted that in South Africa, African National Congress leader

Nelson Mandela had been sentenced to life imprisonment. An air of negativity was spreading; but with a liberalizing element apparent in Europe, that was where the road of opportunity seemed to lead. So, like an earlier generation of American artists in the 1920s, Simon left the USA and looked to Europe, drifting across the Atlantic to France at the beginning of 1964. Behind him he left sporadic teenage triumphs and a growing sense of dissatisfaction. Beyond lay the unknown.

Folk Routes

'If you are lucky enough to have lived in Paris as a young man, then wherever you go for the rest of your life, it stays with you, for Paris is a moveable feast', Ernest Hemingway wrote nostalgically in 1950. On Simon's arrival in 1964, Paris was firmly ensconced in its Fifth Republic, with de Gaulle as its authoritarian head. The Beatles had just finished twenty nights at the Olympia Theatre, their first step on the ladder of world domination, and Paris was a very pop place to be. As a young (temporarily) expatriate American, Simon felt he was a vestige of the Lost Generation of Hemingway, Scott Fitzgerald and Ezra Pound, able to revel in the café society and cultured boulevard conversations; here was an opportunity to forget the whims of the Wobble, legitimately wear a black roll-neck sweater, and pound the tables in pursuit of existentialism and further arguments, fuelled by vin ordinaire.

In Paris, Simon made the most of his 'moveable feast', busking by the Seine, haranguing the boat loads of American tourists who sailed by – they represented the cosy conformity, the superficial 'if it's Tuesday it must be Paris' approach which the bohemian Simon was totally at odds with. It was in Paris that Simon was first introduced to the delights of South American music, the complex and compelling rhythms of Urubamba, and where he also heard Los Incas perform what he would later use as the melody for 'El Condor Pasa'. While based in Paris Simon also followed in Hemingway's footsteps and travelled down to Spain, sleeping at night under Andalucian skies.

Simon could afford to indulge himself in his role as the young, struggling artist, proudly claiming to have slept under a bridge in Paris for a week, but in times of real crisis there was always the American Express office in Paris for succour. Four years later the same American Express office would be attacked by rioting French students during the summer of unrest, when European antagonism to the American involvement in Vietnam led to their most cherished institutions being attacked and vilified. But then, in the innocent, heady days of 1964, Paris provided a bastion for the American abroad, and was a suitably symbolic location for Paul Simon's transition from lone teen-ranger to topical songwriter.

There is some confusion surrounding the genesis of what Simon later called his 'first serious song' – 'He Was My Brother'. The song concerns the murder of three young civil rights activists, Andrew Goodman, Michael Schwerner and James Chaney, who were murdered by the Ku Klux Klan in June 1964 whilst taking part in a negro voter registration drive in Jackson, Mississippi. Art Garfunkel wrote that he first heard the song in 'June 1963, a week after Paul wrote it'.

Despite the confusion over dates, we do know that Simon was profoundly moved by the death of Andy Goodman, a friend of his from acting classes in Queens University days; Simon recalled his reaction on learning of his friend's murder: 'I was in the American Express office in Paris. I had to walk outside. I was going to throw up. I felt dizzy. I was so panicked, so frightened, I couldn't actually believe that anybody I knew was dead. . . . It hit me really hard.' While Simon's latter-day critics consistently try to brand him as a racist, it is worth recalling just how deeply he felt this loss, and how he responded to it by writing a powerful and heartfelt attack on the meat-headed racism of the Klan. The same event also prompted Tom Paxton to write a song, 1965's 'Goodman, Schwerner And Chaney'.

It was whilst in Paris in March 1964 that Simon first met David McLausland, who ran the Brentwood Folk Club in Essex on the outskirts of London, and at his invitation Simon came to London on 11th April, 1964. For millions of young people around the world, London had become the cynosure of all that was stylish – largely thanks to the Beatles. The day that Paul Simon arrived in London, the Fabs were Number 1 with 'Can't Buy Me Love'. Beatlemania was at its height, having effortlessly conquered America, and the world was keen to trace the Beatles phenomenon back to its source: with the capital as their base, London was the focus. In the Beatles' wake came the Rolling Stones, the Yardbirds, The Who, the Animals, the Hollies and hundreds of other new groups from across Great Britain, drawn to the axis of swinging London.

The capital city also boasted a thriving folk scene in the mid-60s, a healthy alternative to the Beat Bonanza which filled Meccas,

Palais's and ABCs up and down the country. There was a buzzing underground circuit of clubs like Les Cousins, Bunjies and the Troubador in London. Al Stewart came up from Bournemouth (after a spell in Tony Blackburn's backing band!), Bert Jansch came down from Glasgow, Sandy Denny came across from Putney and Davey Graham came at it from all angles. They were new young singers, fired by Dylan and his provocative 'finger-pointing' lyrics, determined to bare their souls to thinking audiences who would attentively listen to lyrics, rather than the over-excitable teenagers who screamed so hysterically that they drowned out their own idols.

Talking to me recently, Al Stewart remembered the period: 'A lot of people say Paul Simon or Bert Jansch were looking for a place to play. They couldn't just play the Flamingo or the 100 Club because they wanted bands. . . . I think that myself, and others of my generation, were more or less lured into folk clubs because we played acoustic guitars.' It was in the folk clubs that performers such as the venerable Ewan MacColl, Ian Campbell, Dominic Behan and Alex Campbell were introducing the new, young audiences to the rich melodies and complex narratives of traditional folk music. The effect of Britain's rich folk heritage on visiting American artists such as Dylan, Richard Farina, Tom Paxton, Jackson C. Frank and Carolyn Hester was immediate and lasting; and it was into this creative maelstrom that Paul Simon was plunged in the Easter of 1964.

David Rugg, who ran the Brentwood Folk Club with David McLausland, remembers meeting Simon when he arrived at Heathrow Airport that April, and seeing his performance at the Railway Inn in Brentwood the following night. That first show at Brentwood on Sunday 12th April, 1964 was to have a surprisingly lasting influence on Simon's life. The girl taking tickets on the door was a secretary from Hornchurch in Essex, a friend of Rugg and his future wife Jean, called Kathy. During Simon's eight or so months in Britain, Kathy became his girlfriend and his muse, and would later inspire such classic songs as 'Kathy's Song', 'Homeward Bound' and 'America'.

Simon took a flat in Hampstead, and began working regularly in folk clubs around London, before striking up to the North of England. In his early days playing the London clubs, Simon was already earning £8.10s a night, big money in those days – the well established Martin Carthy was only on £8! Simon was definitely two strokes up on the usual performers who flocked to the folk clubs in the mid-60s: for one thing he wrote and sang his own material, and for another he was American. This was a good time for a young American folkie scudding around Britain – food and drink was cheap, audiences were appreciative, and there was no spectre of Bob Dylan, no immediate yardstick. As recently as 1986, Simon was calling his time in England during 1964/5 'by far my favourite time of my life'.

David Rugg saw Simon perform regularly at that time, a small, compact figure, frequently clad all in black, already a brilliant conveyor of his own intense material: 'He was always well received, especially by people who weren't staunch traditionalists. He definitely appealed to those audiences who went to folk clubs but weren't strictly traditional in their approach to folk music. He had a swinging guitar style, quite jazzy the way he swung, his playing was definitely a cut above his contemporaries. They were quite stilted in their playing, but Paul could easily sing and play guitar well at the same time!' Simon built up a small but effective repertoire of his own material including 'He Was My Brother', 'A Church Is Burning' (another heartfelt swipe at the contemptible Ku Klux Klan), 'A Most Peculiar Man' and 'Sound Of Silence'. His initial impact on British audiences was a strong one, but soon Simon felt impelled to return to his native New York.

Utilizing contacts he had established while scuffing round song publishers a few years before, Simon went back to doing odd jobs around Broadway. This led to the late Tom Wilson of Columbia records hearing his song 'He Was My Brother'. Wilson was impressed with the song and thought it might be right for a folk group he knew called the Pilgrims. Simon insisted, however, that he could do the song more justice with his singing partner Art Garfunkel, who was now teaching in New York following a largely unsuccessful singing career as Artie Garr in the early 60s.

Simon and Garfunkel's 1964 audition for CBS was produced by Roy Halee, who went on to enjoy a fruitful collaboration with the pair throughout their entire career, and after their split helped Simon immeasurably on the *Graceland* project. Garfunkel recalled that even then Halee 'was very much on our side. The next time we had to come back and sing more, the next week, we requested that the guy with the yellow, button-down Oxford shirt be the engineer again!' While his name has come to be inexorably linked with Simon and Garfunkel, Halee's musical pedigree is both impressive and varied. During the 60s he worked on albums with the Byrds, the Lovin' Spoonful and Blood, Sweat and Tears, and he also produced the only album in 1980 of Blue Angel, a promising New York band featuring a singer called Cyndi Lauper.

The audition was a success, and Simon and Garfunkel found themselves on the roster of CBS artists, which at the time included Bob Dylan, Johnny Cash, Andy Williams and Johnny Mathis. Looking back on the circumstances of their signing, Tom Wilson (who was also Dylan's producer until 1965) recalled: 'I started working with these two guys, one who went under the name Jerry Landis and also the name of Paul Kane, and he had a buddy he used to bring round to my office. . . . I said "Why don't we call them Simon and Garfunkel?" And Paul Simon said, "Hey man, people might think we're comedians or something!". . . . Anti-semitism reared its ugly head; he wondered whether people would take issue with the name. So finally, Norman Adler, who was the Executive Vice President, slammed his hand down on the table and said "Gentlemen, this is 1964. Simon and Garfunkel! Next case!"'

At liberty to finally record under their own names without embarrassment, and with the adolescent efforts of seven years before largely forgotten (save for the proud possessors of Roulette's Golden Greats series of albums – 'Hey Schoolgirl' was enshrined on Volume 17!), the two new recording stars in their early twenties could now tackle the serious issues head-on. What is surprising about Simon and Garfunkel's official debut album is the paucity of original material. Throughout his career Simon has never been a prolific writer, but for a debut, particularly at a time when the singer-songwriters in the folk mould were reaching an early zenith, *Wednesday Morning 3 A.M.* was a timid and restrained first effort. Singer and guitarist Barry Kornfeld was a Greenwich Village acquaintance of Simon's, who helped out on the album by playing second guitar alongside acoustic bassist Bill Lee.

Simon and Garfunkel appear on the cover of their debut album as two earnest young men in tidy ties, cautiously eyeing the camera as a subway train thunders by. In fact, as Garfunkel was fond of recounting, the original cover shots for the album had to be scrapped, as every one clearly demonstrated a healthy slice of colourful New York graffiti – while 'the words of the prophets' may well have been written on the subway walls, CBS were plainly unhappy at them being shown on an album cover! The graffiti theme was one which fascinated Simon, and one to which he would return in less than two years for 'A Poem On The Underground Wall'.

Wednesday Morning 3 A.M.'s cover also boasted 'exciting new sounds in the folk tradition', and folk was clearly where the album was aimed, with a version of Dylan's rallying call, 'The Times They Are A–Changin' ', Ed McCurdy's folk standard, 'Last Night I Had The Strangest Dream', and the gospel-style 'Go Tell It On The Mountain'. Ian Campbell's 'The Sun Is Burning' is a song Simon had been impressed by on hearing the composer perform it in England earlier in the year; while Art Garfunkel had unearthed 'Benedictus' in his University library.

Garfunkel's original sleeve notes for the album on its American release in 1964 take the form of an open letter to his partner, who was back in England by the time of the album's release. The album was not issued in Britain until 1968, after Simon and Garfunkel's success with 'Mrs Robinson'; by this time some of Garfunkel's more extravagant prose had been deleted from the sleeve – including his rather fanciful comparison of himself, as Simon's partner, to Kafka's literary executor Max Brod. There still remained some gems of pretension, like the description of Simon's original composition, 'Bleecker Street', in rock-crit terms: 'The second line touches poignantly on human conditions of our times'! But in general, Garfunkel's sleeve notes do provide a fascinating insight into the creation of the five original Paul Simon songs on the album.

Writing of the album over a decade later, Bob Woffinden neatly encapsulated its faults: 'He and Garfunkel . . . clambered aboard the folk bandwagon, borrowing protest from Dylan and harmonies from the Everly Brothers', a point which Robert Shelton also picked up on: 'Essentially, that's what they did with the urban, topical, singer-songwriter protest folk movement. They made it viable and accessible.'

Attempting to tackle the gospel fervour of 'You Can Tell The World' or 'Go Tell It On The Mountain', Simon and Garfunkel lack the necessary passion. The image is of two choirboys, noses pressed against the windows of a Harlem revivalist church. Their version of 'Pretty Peggy-O' (which Dylan had also included on his debut two years before) is reverential. Dylan tackled it like a stray dog gnawing a bone; Simon and Garfunkel forsake the song's narrative drive and development, and their syrupy harmonies are no substitute.

The real heart of the album lies in the five Simon originals. The impact of 'He Was My Brother' was, as with 'Pretty Peggy-O', largely dissipated by the harmonies, and he significantly altered the line *'Mississippi's gonna be your buryin' place'* to *'this town's gonna be*

23

your buryin' place'. 'Sparrow' offers a more rewarding opportunity for flawless harmonizing, although its cumbersome biblical language ('*From dust were ye made and dust ye shall be*') hardly gelled with the contemporary broadsides of Dylan or Ochs. Garfunkel admired the song's prosaic charm, however, and wrote that 'Sparrow' contains 'much of the style that characterizes all the later work'.

'Wednesday Morning 3 A.M.' was inexplicably chosen as the album's title track. What could be Simon's equivalent of a B-movie about a cheap and unnecessary robbery needs to be stark and driving, not reverential and pious; Simon and Garfunkel even manage to make the line about the girl's breasts rising and falling as she sleeps sound unerotic. A better version is the rewritten rock version, which Simon incorporated on the *Sounds of Silence* album two years later under the title 'Somewhere They Can't Find Me'. The song's key line, and one which must cause Simon considerable rueful reflection, is: '*A scene badly written in which I must play*', a view he took of much of the early Simon and Garfunkel material.

'Bleecker Street' is one of the album's undoubted highlights. One of Greenwich Village's main arteries, it ran past all the major folk clubs. From the enticing opening line about the fog rolling in, covering the street like a shroud, through poetic prostitution and betrayal, the song conveys, with acutely observed images, and like a sweeping cinema camera, the time and the place as it then was. Here the biblical imagery is more comfortable, notably in the way that Simon and Garfunkel allow their voices to blend on the line '*it's a long road to Canaan*'. The road that is a return to innocence, Canaan was the land God promised to Abraham for his obedience. It's a New York song from a New York writer just beginning to discover his true voice, with the striking image of voices leaking from a sad café, where only shadowy hands reached out.

In his sleeve notes, Garfunkel delights that 'The Sounds Of Silence' is 'a major work . . . a song on a larger scale'. It took Simon four months to complete, finally falling into place on 19th February, 1964. The title has long since entered common usage, and two passages from the song are among Simon's entries in *The Penguin Dictionary Of Modern Quotations*, along with lines from 'Bridge Over Troubled Water' and 'Mrs Robinson'. He is squeezed in between the authors of 'Yes, We Have No Bananas' and the surrealist playwright N. F. Simpson.

From the chill welcome to darkness in the song's first line, 'The Sounds Of Silence' clearly is, and remains, a major contribution to rock culture, and is perhaps the classic hymn of alienation: an outsider forced to exist in a city from which he draws no comfort, and in which human contact is discouraged – only shadows again. With the vision of the crowd prostrating themselves before '*the neon God they made*', the observer realizes that their downfall is of their own making, their Eden now a neon travesty. Simon, however, as commentator is adrift from the mainstream – '*People writing songs that voices never shared*' is a graphic and touching observation. The inability to communicate, together with the growing cancer of silence, means that those condemned to the silence and isolation of the city have become immunized to their feelings, and are barely able to communicate those feelings to their fellows. Ironically, 'Sounds Of Silence' remains one of the most requested songs in concert – thousands of people baying to hear a song about loneliness and the inability to communicate!

On its release, *Wednesday Morning 3 A.M.* bombed, its first year sales amounting to a meagre 3,000 copies. In retrospect, though, it can still be considered a significant album, if only because it introduced the world to 'The Sounds Of Silence'. By the time it began its nose dive, Paul Simon had again left America behind and returned to Britain; here at least he could be assured of a welcome for his thoughtful and thought-provoking songs.

A Poet and a One-Man-Band

Kathy was waiting for him, and on a professional level Simon was about to meet a redoubtable lady called Judith Piepe, whose championing of his work in Britain during 1964/5 would play a profound part in the development of his career. It was largely due to her tireless work that Simon's songs were ever heard by more than a handful of people in British folk clubs.

Judith had been a social worker in the East End of London since 1962. She was born in Silesia, and her father was a Jewish socialist Member of Parliament, who fled Germany the night the Nazis burnt down the Reichstag in 1933. She met Paul Simon first after seeing him perform at the Flamingo Club in Wardour Street one evening late in 1964, when the headline act had failed to turn up. She remembers Simon performing 'A Church Is Burning', 'The Leaves That Are Green' and 'The Sounds Of Silence' to a great response: so great that Simon asked Art Garfunkel, who was holidaying in Europe at the time, to join him on stage. The pair sang a flawless 'Benedictus'. Judith was completely overwhelmed by the content of the songs and the duo's ability to put across their nuances in performance, and virtually single-handedly she began a campaign to get Paul Simon recognized and established as a major talent.

Simon spent a generous slice of 1964 in Britain, appearing down the bill at the Edinburgh and Cambridge Folk Festivals. Folk singer and broadcaster Wally Whyton remembers meeting Simon in England at that time; he and Redd Sullivan and Simon had been double booked at a folk club in Chelmsford: 'He came in as high as a kite and the three of us ended up doing a whole evening of rock and roll . . . Leiber and Stoller, the Coasters, 'Dream Lover' and stuff. There was no folk music *that* night! But then, I didn't think there was ever any question of Paul and *folk* music.' A point which Hugh Jones of Liverpool folk quartet the Spinners reinforced: 'I remember seeing him at the Troubador, and at a club in Widnes, but we

26

didn't book him. He was a beautiful player and singer, but nothing to do with folk music, and we were *very* folkie in those days.' Playwright Willy Russell, author of *John, Paul, George, Ringo and Bert* and *Educating Rita*, also recalls the young Simon at work in the Cross Keys in Liverpool: 'He was in this very casual, determinedly amateur environment, whereas he was very sophisticated and professional and doing an *act*, which was shunned in English folk clubs!'

While in England in 1964, Simon adopted another alias, that of Paul Kane, taking his surname from Charles Foster of that ilk in Orson Welles' cinematic masterpiece *Citizen Kane*. The name change was undertaken for purely commercial reasons – he was under contract to CBS as half of Simon and Garfunkel, but keen to make some more money and gain further mileage from his songs.

Not surprisingly, confusion arises when you try to pin down who was the first artist in Britain to record a Paul Simon/Paul Kane song. Folk singer Harvey Andrews remembers seeing Simon perform in Birmingham in 1964 and being blown away by his performance which centred on 'A Church Is Burning', 'A Most Peculiar Man', 'He Was My Brother' and 'The Sounds of Silence' – 'I'd never seen or heard anything like it, he was such a one-man band, an astonishing guitarist.' Andrews, who was just beginning his own career, was so impressed by Simon's song about a suicide, 'A Most Peculiar Man', that he included it on his debut EP and hailed Simon as 'the next Dylan'.

Another strand is added with the entrance of Irish singer Val Doonican; nowadays an almost permanent fixture on British television in his trademark sweaters and rocking chair, back in 1964 Doonican was a struggling young singer, whose big break with 'Walk Tall' in October 1964 was still to come. His song publisher, the late Alan Paramour (brother of Cliff Richard and the Shadows' producer Norrie Paramour), played Doonican a Kane song, 'Carlos Dominguez', 'a Mexican type thing', Doonican remembers, which he included on his first album. 'Citizen Kane' himself also recorded the song in 1964, backed with 'He Was My Brother', on the long-gone Oriole label, but it remains one of his more obscure songs of the period. It borrows its construction from the folk ballad 'question and answer' structure, with Simon as the song's narrator asking Carlos Dominguez (*'an unhappy man'*) just why he's so unhappy. The ambitious Señor Dominguez is merely searching for peace of mind, truth, answers and love. It's an obvious Simon song of the period, full of questions but with no answers provided.

Simon still considers the period he spent bumming round the folk clubs in Britain in the mid-60s as a golden one, and the effect on his songwriting was substantial; his major 'selling point' to audiences who were used to interminable sea shanties and Dylan covers was the profound and unsettling nature of his original songs. He told Michael Parkinson in 1975 about those early songs crafted in Britain: 'They have a sort of innocence, which is what is nice about them. You write about when you're scruffy, you're poor, you're travelling round, that's fine subject matter for a song. Then, if you start having hits, it's not an interesting subject for a song – "I live in a big house" is boring, and liable to antagonize a lot of people.' It was in Britain that Simon found being a native New Yorker had its advantages: 'I was just a Jewish kid from Queens', he told David Hepworth in 1986, 'Paxton came from Oklahoma, Dylan was from Minnesota. I was simply not from far enough away to make it in the Village. But when I was here I was strange because I was American.'

Using London as his base, Simon tore around Britain and played a string of folk club dates in the north. It was while waiting on Widnes station platform for the milk train back to London that Paul Simon began writing 'Homeward Bound'; sad at being away from his Kathy, worried that his songs would come back and haunt him *'in shades of mediocrity'*, it remains one of the rock and roll road's finest milestones.

Judith Piepe's exposure to Simon's songs at the Flamingo had left her convinced that Simon was destined to become a major figure in the popular music establishment. However, record companies displayed a familiar disinterest and even Alan Paramour, who was handling Simon's publishing at Lorna Music and was fond of the young writer, had little faith. He confided to Judith: 'He's a nice little boy, but of course these songs are far too intellectual and too uncommercial.' But Judith was undeterred and switched her attention to the august BBC. In 1964 pop music had some outlet on the Light Programme but it was to be three years before they succumbed to the influence of the pirate stations and delivered bright, breezy, national Radio 1. After the Flamingo gig, Judith learnt that Paul was returning to the States to go back to college; Curly Goss at the Flamingo promised Paul some gigs in early 1965 and Judith promised she would champion his work in his absence, and he agreed to return to London for a week in January 1965. Judith remembered that period for me seventeen years later: 'I plagued the BBC and said, "There is a young American songwriter and he is *the* songwriter of our time and something's got to stay here before he goes again. He's only in England for seven days." I just drove them mad. So finally they said, "All right, he can have a studio for an hour." '

On Simon's return to Britain in January 1965, virtually his first stop was at the BBC studio, where in the space of an hour, with Judith supervising, he recorded twelve of his own songs: 'But nobody there knew what to do with them', remembered Judith. 'The Home Service said it wasn't family entertainment. The Light Programme said it wasn't light enough and the Third Programme said it wasn't classical enough!' Quite where the songs of Paul Simon could slot into the strictly hierarchical BBC was a problem, but Judith's tenacity and ingenuity ensured that the tape found its way round Broadcasting House and eventually wound up in the unlikely offices of Religious Broadcasting. *Five to Ten* was a brief slot sandwiched between *Housewives' Choice* and *Workers' Playtime*, in which clerics would impart their thoughts for the day to the listening housewife and worker. The usual line-up consisted of a pertinent fable, a hymn and a prayer, but Judith ingeniously arranged the dozen songs into three groups, which she entitled 'Songs of the Brotherhood of Man', 'Songs of the Loneliness of Men' and 'More Songs by Paul Simon'. They were broadcast over a fortnight, with an introduction by Judith each day: 'They were probably overtly less religious than anything they had ever had, but the songs were to do with people, with life. . . . The first one I started off by saying, "Do you spend any time in the pubs, clubs or coffee bars of Soho? Or do your kids, if they tell you, that is?" But it was the second one, "A Church Is Burning", when I said, "A church that isn't worth setting on fire isn't worth calling a church!". . . . The head of Religious Broadcasting was horrified. . . . It totally changed religious broadcasting, it never went back to the old format.'

The effect of Simon's twelve songs was immediate. Judith was inundated with letters, particularly from 'radical priests' who wrote, 'I don't normally listen to this programme, *but* . . .!' The *Five to Ten* broadcasts even led to a short book by Tony Jasper, *The Religious Content of Paul Simon's Songs*. Naturally among the many letters Judith received after the broadcasts were inquiries about where versions could be obtained on record, and that gave Paul and Judith a lever with which to approach record companies.

CBS London were just beginning to make their mark as an independent operation in Europe, and somewhat grudgingly they took up the option; accordingly, in May 1965, Paul Simon entered

Levy's Studio in Bond Street with his £90 advance to record his first solo album *The Paul Simon Songbook*. It featured all the songs broadcast on *Five to Ten* save one – 'Bad News Feeling' – which Simon has never officially released. It was a song dealing with the young drug addicts in the East End with whom Judith Piepe was in daily contact, and had a tune lightly based on Davey Graham's 'Anji'. It was a minor work, the solitary Simon *'leaving home, vaguely stoned'* and reflecting that the *real* bad news feeling is having no feelings at all.

The whole album was recorded in barely an hour at a total cost of £60, with one microphone deemed sufficient for the purpose, so that on 'The Sound Of Silence' you can hear Simon stamping his foot in time to the music. The acknowledgement of two producers, Stanley West and Reginald Warburton, belies the innate simplicity of the album. West was a hangover from Simon's Oriole contract, while Warburton was the producer CBS assigned to the album; but Judith remembered their input as being minimal.

Simon had been playing the twelve songs endlessly across the length and breadth of the British Isles, so that when the time came to make the album, only one take was needed for each song. It is that confidence in his material and the clearly felt need to make it on his own terms that lends the album its importance. The songs on it formed the basis of Simon and Garfunkel's repertoire for many years, and indeed many of them – 'I Am A Rock', 'The Sound of Silence', 'Kathy's Song' and 'April Come She Will' – remain among the composer's best-known and finest works.

In later years Simon had CBS delete the album, seemingly as part of his attempt to obfuscate his past. Curious though, because while *The Paul Simon Songbook* may not show the slick professionalism which became his hallmark, it is nonetheless a rich and rewarding set. Simon's performance infuses the songs with an urgency and intensity only found in the young and hungry; he was determined to make his mark with what could well be his only shot.

The stark presentation of the songs means that they have to stand or fall on their own merits and Simon's interpretation of them; no faults or inherent weaknesses can be disguised by production gloss. Despite the many subsequent versions of 'The Sound Of Silence', for example, the finest on record remains this version on the *Songbook*; Simon had only been living with the song for just over a year, and there is none of the weariness or jaundiced performance which would come in later years. It stands as a version by the composer, justifiably proud of his creation and still finding his way round the song – hear him attack the penultimate verse as he castigates the fools who do not know.

Even the poetically petulant 'I Am A Rock' – about an outsider surrounded by his books and poetry to 'protect' him – is effectively handled here; (Wally Whyton remembers Simon previously being very impressed by a Derrol Adams song, 'I Wish I Was A Rock'). While the 'major works' are maturely handled, it is the love songs which are most engaging – 'The Leaves That Are Green' and 'April Come She Will' draw much from English traditional ballads, while 'Kathy's Song' remains Simon's finest ever love song, painting him as human and vulnerable without resorting to the cultivated isolation which would colour his later works. It is Kathy who is pictured on the album cover on the *'narrow streets of cobblestone'*, toying with Gonks, those curiously popular relics of the 1960s. Judith Piepe remembered her as 'the silent haiku. Kathy was lovely . . . she's the silent love of "Homeward Bound" and "America" . . . she was very special. Every songwriter should have a Kathy.'

Among the other songs on the album, 'A Simple Desultory Philippic' – which Simon would subsequently update on the *Parsley, Sage, Rosemary and Thyme* album the following year – is an affectionate satire. The 1966 version was an acerbic put-down, but in 1965 the song was gentler, very much a product of his time in England, with references to Union Jacks, Rolls Royces and Diz Disley (an excellent guitarist and stalwart of the British folk and jazz scenes). *'It's all right Ma, it's something I learned over in England'* is Simon having a dig at Dylan, who originated the line on his song 'I Shall Be Free No. 10' on his fourth album.

Simon's performance of 'He Was My Brother' is streets ahead of the version that appeared on the *Wednesday Morning* album. Simon sings with sincerity, and with the loss of Garfunkel's harmonies the song has much more punch. In fact, one of the main strengths of the *Songbook* is that the power of the songs is not diluted by Garfunkel's angelic voice. 'The Side Of A Hill' is a childishly effective anti-war song; with 'a little cloud weeping' it recalls the naive charm of 'Leaves That Are Green'. Never one to throw anything away, Simon incorporated the song as the 'Canticle' section of 'Scarborough Fair' a year later.

One curious aspect of the album is Simon's own disparaging sleeve notes (an art he would forsake until *Graceland* over twenty years later). Considering that the songs contained therein are the fruits of Simon's first solo work, and contain some of his most important and mature songs, his reflections on them are strangely dismissive: 'This LP contains twelve of the songs that I have written over the past two years. There are some here that I would not write today. I don't believe in them as I once did. I have included them because they played an important role in the transition.' But *which* transition? From Jerry Landis to Paul Simon? From Tico (not forgetting the Triumphs) to Paul Kane? From failed teenage prodigy to fledgling folk singer? Whatever the confusion in Simon's mind, the resultant album was a delight to him, as he told David Hepworth in 1986: 'To be twenty-two years old and to have your girlfriend on your album cover. That was *it!*'

The album sales were disappointing but nevertheless *The Paul Simon Songbook* remains the best souvenir of Simon's fruitful years in England. The songs are as much works in progress as finished pieces; Simon is testing himself and his material, pitching in with an urgency and commitment which is fully justified by the end result. For anyone remotely interested in the development of Paul Simon's career, the *Songbook* is vital to a fuller understanding of where he had come from and where he was going.

For all its excellence, one can understand Simon's attitude to his first solo album. The songs were all quite old by the time he came to record them; the love songs aside, they deal with Simon's fascination for isolation and the inability to communicate. Simon was in danger of finding himself typecast like Colin Wilson had with his first book, *The Outsider*, a decade before. But for Paul Simon in England that summer of 1965, life was far removed from the bleak isolation of his songs, he had a good following and career in the British folk clubs, the lovely, inspirational Kathy close by, and his own album in the record shops.

England Swings

'I first met Paul when I was nineteen in the spring of 1965', Al Stewart told me in 1987. 'We were both living in Judith Piepe's flat in the East End. I remember the first time we actually spoke, I bumped into him and said, "What do you do?" He said, "I write songs," and played me "Flowers Never Bend with the Rainfall", whch I thought owed a lot to the Beatles . . . looking back, it was a great place to live then – Paul and Artie were staying there, Jackson C. Frank was staying there with his girlfriend Sandy Denny. Judith had this ability to attract all the stray dogs.'

Simon and Garfunkel went on to their own fair share of fame, and the late and sadly missed Sandy Denny went on to guide Fairport Convention through their halcyon period, but the real joker in the pack was the American Jackson C. Frank. Bert Jansch once told me that Frank was as much an influence on the English folk scene as Bob Dylan (indeed Roy Harper commemorated him in song on 'My Friend', as did Sandy Denny with 'Next Time Around'), but save for a few die-hard devotees his name is largely unknown. This has as much to do with his own mercurial character as it does with the paucity of his recorded work. He only ever released one album, *Jackson C. Frank*, on EMI in 1965. The album was produced by Paul Simon – still one of his few 'outside' production credits – with second guitar from Al Stewart, who remembers the enigmatic Frank as being 'an extraordinary character. He'd been very badly burned in a fire in the States, and received something like $100,000 compensation, which he promptly blew on cars. I remember he had an Aston Martin and a Bentley when I knew him!'

Simon spent £30 of his CBS advance on recording the Frank album, which was all done in three hours. Al Stewart remembers the session: 'Paul asked me to play guitar . . . for which he never paid me, although Jackson bought me lunch! Artie was the tea boy

33

at the session! . . . Jackson just froze in the studio. I remember him saying to Paul, "I can't play – you're *looking* at me", which made the producer's role rather difficult! Eventually, we sort of erected some screens around him to shield him from the gaze of the control room. We only actually got him to record by Paul asking him to play for levels – he managed to get five songs that way!'

The album when released sank without trace, selling barely 1,000 copies, although it has since then justifiably accrued a cult reputation. 'Blues Run The Game', the album's opening track, is a classic of the period, and Frank's other nine songs certainly display a talented individual who never reached the audience he deserved. *Jackson C. Frank* was subsequently reissued in 1978 – with no producer's credit – and included a fascinating open letter from Frank, which gives an interesting insight into the dilemma faced by American singer-songwriters like Frank and Simon in London in the mid–60s. Frank wrote: 'I had just begun writing songs consistently at that point. I still remember someone saying, "Well, you are a singer-songwriter. Why didn't you stay in America? Look at Dylan!" And I replied "The reason I *didn't* stay was that I looked at Dylan." '

Al Stewart to this day retains fond memories of his associations with Simon back then; he watched Simon work the clubs and learnt from him about stagecraft and handling audiences. Stewart also remembers Simon honing the Widnes-inspired song of early 1965: 'I was in the next room at the flat when he wrote "Homeward Bound". It took him three hours. Soon after that he played me "Richard Cory", and I told him *that* was the one – forget about "Homeward Bound"!'

Covers of his songs by Harvey Andrews and Val Doonican, however gratifying, were not the stuff of Simon's dreams: 'One day he asked me if I had £5,000', laughed Al Stewart, 'I didn't have 5,000 pennies then. He wanted the money because he was keen to sell his entire song catalogue, which included "Sounds Of Silence" and "Homeward Bound". We spent an entire afternoon walking round Tin Pan Alley, Denmark Street, but none of the publishers were interested.'

Simon explored another avenue with the help of Lorna Music's Alan Paramour, who introduced him to Bruce Woodley of the Seekers, the clean-cut Australian quartet then at the peak of their success with their winsome folk-based melodies. Simon and Woodley hit it off well enough to collaborate on a number of songs, two of which – 'Red Rubber Ball' and 'I Wish You Could Be Here'

– appeared on the Seekers' 1966 album, *Come The Day*. The pair also wrote a song 'Someday, One Day', which gave the Seekers a further hit in Britain in March 1966 when it reached Number 11. 'Red Rubber Ball' was a major hit for the American group the Cyrkle in the early summer of 1966, the only US act managed, briefly, by Brian Epstein. Simon and Woodley were a short-lived partnership, but the songs they wrote together had all the hallmarks one associates with Simon's best work of the period. 'I Wish You Could Be Here' is a particularly haunting ballad, an atmospheric piece which evokes a really intimate sense of place and time at the ending of a relationship, with lines like: '*The crackle of the fire is laughing in my ear/I've got lots of empty time to kill and I wish you could be here.*'

Simon was managing to make a living out of his music and during 1965 he and Kathy undertook a cross-country holiday in the USA, which would later form the basis of the 1968 song 'America'. In the folk clubs, Simon would perform his own songs with an intensity few could match, throwing in the odd Everly Brothers song for light relief, and other punters can remember him running through songs like Tom Paxton's 'Can't Help But Wonder Where I'm Bound', some token Woody Guthrie material and traditional songs like 'The House Carpenter' culled from Joan Baez albums.

In 1965, as well as performing with Art Garfunkel in a concert arranged by Judith Piepe for the inmates of Brixton Prison, Simon also managed a solo slot on the prestigious *Ready, Steady, Go* in July. He was asked to perform a truncated 'I Am A Rock' to ensure that P. J. Proby could sing *all* his current hit 'Let The Water Run Down'; Simon felt his song was more important, and having weighed up the consequences he sang it straight through, which saw the pony-tailed Proby cut off in mid-song!

Simon still played from time to time at Brentwood and David Rugg remembers him as 'quite a friendly chap . . . a liberal young American, quite typical of the type around at that time. He definitely wasn't a Marxist, but politically okay, strongly against racism, he was quite outspoken in conversation and in his songs about racism in the deep South at home.'

When not playing the folk clubs, Simon would be out most nights watching his contemporaries at work. He was particularly impressed with a guitar piece by the eclectic Davey Graham called 'Anji'. Al Stewart: 'Just remembering back at the flat in 1965, Paul *always* seemed to play "Anji". Every time he picked up the guitar, he seemed obsessed by it and of course included it on the *Sounds of*

Silence album. Just hearing "Anji" always reminds me of Paul and the flat back then.' The flat was in Cable Street at the heart of the East End, the site of violent clashes thirty years before between Oswald Mosley's fascist Blackshirts and residents who violently rejected Mosley's Nazi tactics in the bitter street battles of the mid-30s.

After failing to sell his song catalogue, Simon didn't have much luck with engaging managers either; the late Tony Stratton-Smith, founder of Charisma Records and father figure of Genesis and Peter Gabriel, refused to look after him at this time, giving as his excuse that he 'couldn't handle singer-songwriters'. Strat wasn't alone in his ambivalence towards Simon; Tony Molyneux, who ran the Southport Folk Club, remembered him at that time: 'I wasn't very impressed with his songs, his patter or his seeming arrogance. I thought he was rather a conceited man, which came over in his songs. We had a chance to book him at £8, but that was rather expensive in those days and we turned him down. . . . I certainly didn't put him in the same class as Tom Paxton, Phil Ochs etc, who had more meaningful songs and stronger tunes in my opinion.'

John Whelan, who was in the folk-rock band the Compromise at the time and a regular on the London folk circuit, remembered Paul Simon around then: 'Long John Baldry, who was then immensely popular around the clubs, had dropped into Cousins for an acoustic blues set, after headlining at the Marquee or somewhere earlier in the evening. I remember there was a loud altercation on the stairs; this tiny guy with his guitar, shouting that he'd been booked and what the fuck was Baldry doing here? There was a lot of bad feeling about this guy bad-mouthing Baldry and you could sense the audience's feeling of "all right – show me" when Simon eventually got on stage. That kind of arrogance wasn't welcomed at Cousins, but when he started playing, from the first song – "Sounds of Silence" I think – he won the crowd over immediately.'

Martin Carthy, then already well on the way to becoming the single most influential and innovative figure on the British folk scene – a position he has tenaciously maintained over the years – was another who remained unconverted. While recognizing Simon's talent, his view was soured by Simon's claim to have written a song called 'Scarborough Fair'. Carthy had included the song on his debut album *Martin Carthy* in 1965, and remembers learning it from a Ewan MacColl and Peggy Seeger songbook *The Singing Island*: 'It was never my song, it was there for anybody to do. The only thing I resent is that he said he wrote it. He took enormous pains to learn it when I wrote it down word for word for him. It's as much his song as it was mine, but his way of getting it wasn't entirely honourable I think.'

Carthy was then, as now, a dedicated singer and unearther of traditional material; he had been a great help and source of inspiration to Bob Dylan on his visit to Britain in 1962 (a fact Dylan acknowledged on the sleeve of *Freewheelin'*, remembering that he got the tune for 'Bob Dylan's Dream' from hearing Carthy sing the traditional 'Lord Franklin'). Carthy's label Fontana, although more interested in their Top 20 pop acts such as Marianne Faithfull and Wayne Fontana, had even been keen to release Carthy's version of 'Scarborough Fair' as a single, but he refused: 'I don't really believe my version would have made me $20 million or whatever, or that it would have led me to do the music for *The Graduate*!' But many of Simon's contemporaries on the folk scene resented the fact that when 'Scarborough Fair' did appear on *Parsley, Sage, Rosemary and Thyme* in 1966, it did not carry the token 'Trad. Arr. Paul Simon'; the composing credit led many to believe it was an original song.

Judith Piepe defiantly counters Carthy's tale. She remembered an American student called Caroline Culpepper staying at her flat and teaching Art Garfunkel how to play guitar; one of the songs she remembers Garfunkel learning was 'Scarborough Fair': 'I know that Martin Carthy said that Paul had stolen the accompaniment from him. This is not true. . . . It is possible that Caroline had picked up Martin's accompaniment, it is possible that some of it came that way. . . . I know that when Artie learned it from Caroline, Martin Carthy was nowhere near.'

Even in England Simon had not completely escaped the spectre of Bob Dylan. In September 1965, the widely respected folklorist and singer Ewan MacColl railed against Dylan's folk-rock songs in *Melody Maker*, calling them 'old hat' and lacking 'real anger', even comparing them to the lumbering old radio soap opera *Mrs Dale's Diary*. The following week *Melody Maker* carried a comment from 'American folk singer' Paul Simon, who agreed with MacColl's attack, saying he found 'Dylan's poetry . . . punk (!) and old hat. I think it is just rehashed Ginsberg.'

Al Stewart also remembers Simon's antipathy to Dylan: 'I had a furious argument with Paul about Bob Dylan. *Highway 61 Revisited* was just about to be released and I got a copy on the Wednesday, two days before its official release, and locked myself in my room for two days learning "Desolation Row", which was quite a feat because as you know it's eleven minutes long. Paul wandered in while "Tombstone Blues" was playing, that bit about *"the city fathers trying to endorse the reincarnation of Paul Revere's horse!"* He said "That's rubbish". I made him sit down and listen to "Desolation Row", which to his credit he did for all eleven minutes. I said, "This is *fantastic!*" He said "It's rehashed Ferlinghetti", who I hadn't actually heard of, but I felt I had to respond and snapped back, "The day you live to write a song as good as that is the day you live to be four million years old!" He didn't talk to me for a month!'

Despite some bad feelings from folk club organizers and performers, Simon's reputation with audiences was now well established and his future as a stranger in a strange land looked secure, but Simon's English idyll would not last for much longer. Wally Whyton remembers the last time he saw Simon before he went back to America: 'He turned up at a club, out of the blue, in a white Sunbeam Alpine, seven hundred quids-worth of sports car, when we were all running around in old Ford Anglias. He never said where he got the money from but I assume it must have been the first royalty cheque.'

Many people have latterly accused Simon of 'using' the folk clubs as a deliberate first step on the ladder of success, which is nonsense. The clubs were a forum for exchanging ideas and learning songs. While they may not have had the camaraderie of Greenwich Village, British folk clubs of the period were an invaluable platform. Everyone, unless they were forging a name on the Beat circuit, was 'using' the folk clubs as a stepping stone. By choice, major figures such as Martin Carthy still prefer the intimacy and knowledgeable audiences that the clubs can attract. Bob Dylan, Richard Farina, Tom Paxton and Jackson C. Frank also 'used' the folk clubs, as did Bert Jansch and John Renbourne; so did Sandy Denny, Tom Robinson and even Elvis Costello, until their own shining talents swiftly outgrew the tiny venues.

Like most young ambitious musicians, Simon was always hustling journalists to get his name in print. Chris Welch of *Melody Maker* was used to seeing Simon tearing around London with his guitar case: 'It's funny, thinking back, he was quite often seen around the pubs where the music journalists congregated, like the Red Lion in Fleet Street. . . . I was in the White Lion by Centre Point one lunch-time and saw him come in, and dodged out of the pub to avoid being buttonholed, saying, "Oh God, here comes Paul Simon again!" Hard to believe that at one time I deliberately tried to avoid Paul Simon.' Wally Whyton also spoke to me about the end of Simon's time in London during 1965: 'I think what we could give him was a very minute part of what he wanted, therefore he didn't demand a lot from us. I think he realized that folk clubs were a blind alley, but on the other hand, it was a way of meeting audiences.'

In 1965, Alan Smith of the *New Musical Express* conducted an interview with Simon which wasn't even published until three years later when Simon and Garfunkel were breaking with 'Mrs Robinson'. The interview gives a portrait of Simon as a contented folkie happily scuffing round the British folk clubs; with two albums to his name, and a modest future in Britain looking assured, Simon, true to his image, shunned the pop scene as he felt it stifled creativity and 'encouraged freaks'. The interview concludes with Simon's humble ambitions: 'All I need is somewhere to eat and sleep and buy guitar strings. I haven't any real need for money, so I've made out okay.' He was twenty-four years old. Presciently Smith asked him how he would cope with hit records, anathema to the creative artist? 'Well . . . I've never had a hit, although over in the states right now, a song of mine called "Sounds of Silence" is beginning to move. . . .'

So, it quickly turned out, was Paul Simon!

Homeward Bound

It is ironic that the two men to whom Paul Simon owes his permanent success remain anonymous. It was a nameless Boston disc jockey who spontaneously lifted Simon and Garfunkel's acoustic verison of 'Sounds of Silence' from *Wednesday Morning 3 A.M.*, and began programming it into his show over a period of weeks during 1965, keenly gauging reaction from the students at nearby Harvard and Tufts university campuses. The response was positive, positive enough to make the local CBS promotion man realize that there was some commercial mileage to be gained from a largely forgotten song by one of his label's less commercial acts. He duly notified the label headquarters in New York, and the rest, as they say, is history.

Throughout 1965, folk-rock suddenly became a marketable commodity – pertinent, topical lyrics grafted onto an electric Beat backing. To the chagrin of the folk establishment, it was Bob Dylan who had taken the precipitous first step; his landmark albums *Bringing It All Back Home* in March and *Highway 61 Revisited* in August had been bitterly divisive, but commercially acceptable. As with so much during that time, where Dylan led, numerous imitators were quick to follow. It took the Byrds – an otherwise unremarkable west coast band inspired by the Beatles – to give Dylan's work the sheen of success, when their electric version of 'Mr Tambourine Man' raced to the Number 1 slot in Britain and America in the summer of 1965. 'Like A Rolling Stone' gave Dylan his own biggest hit and soon folk-rock fusionists Barry McGuire ('Eve Of Destruction') and Sonny and Cher ('I Got You Babe') were suddenly Number 1 acts. It's an old record company adage that once the market is identified you tap the vein dry as quickly as possible! From such commercial mining some good and durable music did come; the good-time east coast jugband sound of the Lovin' Spoonful, the flawless west coast harmonies of the Mamas and the Papas . . . and the electric version of Simon and Garfunkel's 'Sounds of Silence'.

With regional interest in the song growing, CBS approached Tom Wilson – Simon and Garfunkel's producer and also the man who had helped steer Dylan towards electricity on his two seminal albums – with a view to giving the song a more folk-*rock* sound to cash in on the summer's craze. Wilson used the same band who had worked with Dylan, and overdubbed bass, drums and electric guitar onto Simon and Garfunkel's original acoustic track to beef it up.

Needless to say, neither of the original artists were even consulted. Art Garfunkel had virtually given up music, singing only occasionally at Gerde's Folk City in New York, but concentrating on obtaining his master's degree from Columbia University, while Paul Simon was drifting round the folk clubs in Europe. Simon was actually in Denmark in September 1965, when he chanced upon a copy of the trade paper *Billboard* and to his amazement noticed a song called 'The Sounds Of Silence' in the lower reaches of the Hot 100. Nearly twenty years later, Simon recalled that as he went on stage to play a Danish folk club gig, with that copy of *Billboard* at hand, he realized that life would never be the same again for him. Returning to the Cable Street flat, Simon immediately contacted Garfunkel to try and map out their future.

A few days later Al Stewart was there when: 'Tom Wilson mailed an electric copy of 'Sounds Of Silence' to Paul, who was *horrified* when he first heard it. In fact, if you listen to that original version you can hear the rhythm section slow down at one point so that Paul and Artie's voices can catch up. . . . The single went in at something like 86 then up into the 30s on the second week, and Columbia rang Paul to say, "It's going to be Number 1."'

Surprisingly, 'The Sounds Of Silence' was never a hit for Simon and Garfunkel in Britain; Simon was particularly scathing about the version that did hit in Britain three months later. The Bachelors were an anachronism, an Irish trio who enjoyed a vogue in Britain at the height of the Beat boom; three forever smiling Irish lads with a penchant for ersatz ballads which appealed to the mums and dads. Their version of 'Sounds Of Silence' was a singularly unsympathetic one and was followed by another song in the folk-rock protest vein – 'Hello Dolly'!

Plugged into the new sound of folk-rock, 'Sounds Of Silence' raced to the US Number 1 slot just prior to Christmas 1965. For Paul Simon the event was a watershed in his career. He was twenty-four years old, earning a comfortable, fairly anonymous living as a solo folk singer in Europe where he had achieved a small degree of fame. Garfunkel had long since resigned himself to a life of academic anonymity, but now, thanks to the tinkerings of Tom Wilson, they found themselves forcibly reunited as Simon and Garfunkel, a public duo which would become synonymous with sound quality and lyrical perception in popular music for the rest of the decade.

It was now essential to acquire a public face, but it was a task which Paul approached with a noticeable lack of relish. At the beginning of 1965 when Simon had returned to Europe he was still struggling to make it as a solo performer, and the only place where that looked likely to happen was in the closed and parochial world of the folk clubs. Less than a year later he was returning to America as a star with a Number 1 hit record. There were hurried farewells to friends in England and vague promises to return.

Back in a bitterly cold New York in time for Christmas, Simon returned to the family home and thrived on the neighbourhood's renewed interest in their local pop star – it was almost exactly eight years since 'Hey Schoolgirl' had provoked earlier interest. He later remembered sharing a joint with Garfunkel on a Queens street corner, musing over the unreality of the situation, as he told *Playboy*: 'I remember Artie and I were sitting there in my car . . . and the announcer said "Number 1, Simon and Garfunkel", and Artie said to me, "That Simon and Garfunkel, they must be having a great time!" '

With vivid memories of their Tom and Jerry days, Simon and Garfunkel knew just how voracious and demanding the record industry could be. Back then in the 60s pop music was already big business, with the stress on making it, getting as much out of it as you could, then mutating into an 'all-round entertainer'. The Beatles and Bob Dylan had shown that pop music could be a legitimate creative vehicle, but on a business level they were incredibly shabbily treated. Just consider the Beatles at the apogee of their success, and look at a typical itinerary for their years at the height of Beatlemania – at least two British and American tours, three new singles and two LPs each year! If Brian Epstein couldn't see just how durable a property the Beatles were going to be, then what chance did a couple of newcomers called Simon and Garfunkel have?

True to form, CBS insisted that the duo capitalize on their success immediately, and in December 1965 their second album, *Sounds Of Silence*, was recorded on the run, over a three-week period at the CBS Los Angeles and Nashville studios, while the single was still holding down the top slot. The album was, in effect, a cobbled together, electric reworking of *The Paul Simon Songbook*; six of the songs from Simon's solo debut cropped up again, and Garfunkel's contribution to the album seems to be minimal; chiefly noticeable is his beautiful handling of 'April Come She Will'.

Naturally, their best-known song, 'Sounds Of Silence', became the album's title track; it was the third time the composer had used it on an album in barely eighteen months. The whole song appears on a further four albums, and a snatch can even be heard on *Bookends*. As to the actual title, the rule of thumb seems to be that when it is Paul Simon performing it, it is 'The Sound Of Silence', but when he's joined by Art Garfunkel it's 'Sound*s*'. Even their record company seem somewhat confused on this point, as on the sleeve of the *Wednesday Morning* album it's 'The Sounds . . .', but on the actual label it's singular!

There were only four brand new Paul Simon songs on the album. 'Blessed' was written when Simon was staying at Judith Piepe's flat. He had once taken shelter in St Anne's Church in Soho during a thunderstorm and was inspired to write a song against religious cant and hypocrisy. The British singer Guy Darrell later covered the song and released it as an unsuccessful single in 1966. Simon was gratified that his songs were attracting attention, but reasoned that because of the 'way out' lyrics, Darrell's single wouldn't get any airplay. He was right, it sank without trace. 'We've Got A Groovey Thing Goin'', as its title implies, is hardly a major work and recalls the frivolity of the Tom and Jerry days.

'Richard Cory' was based on a poem by the nineteenth-century poet Edward Arlington Robinson (*Mr* Robinson?); the original sixteen-line poem concluded: '*And Richard Cory, one calm summer night/Went home and put a bullet through his head.*' Simon used this as the basis for an exposition on power and wealth. Years later Denny Laine would feature 'Richard Cory' regularly on stage when he was a member of Paul McCartney's Wings; the best version of the song, however, is the one by the Belfast group Them, featuring a brooding vocal from the young Van Morrison.

'Richard Cory' is followed on the album by another song about a suicide, but one from the opposite end of the social scale. 'A Most Peculiar Man' was another song from London (and had already appeared on the *Songbook*); Judith Piepe remembers Simon reading a sadly sparse newspaper report of a suicide which concluded with the dead man's landlady commenting that he had been 'a most peculiar man'. 'Paul thought it wasn't enough, so he sat down and wrote an epitaph for a stranger, and for all outsiders.'

The album's major new work, 'Homeward Bound', was released as Simon and Garfunkel's second single and became a US Top 10 hit in March 1966. It remains one of the truest and most haunting evocations of life on the road. Despite innumerable hearings in concert and on record, it still stands as one of Simon's most poignant songs, brilliantly capturing that period of his life when home was London, where he knew he would find his friends and Kathy.

One of the very few cover versions ever to appear on a Simon and Garfunkel album was Davey Graham's 'Anji', a ferociously complex piece which Simon had picked up in London and recorded on *Sounds Of Silence* to give the ailing Graham some badly needed royalties. 'Somewhere They Can't Find Me' – a hastily rewritten electric version of 'Wednesday Morning 3 A.M.' – has a guitar introduction which also owes more than a nod to 'Anji'.

'I Am A Rock' was the third single to be lifted off the album, and became Simon and Garfunkel's third Top 10 hit in less than a year, when it reached Number 3 in America during the summer of 1966. The duo were now firmly established as a force to be reckoned with. The success of 'I Am A Rock' may have been the final necessary proof that 'The Sounds Of Silence' had not been a fluke, but it is one of Simon's weakest ever songs, overdosing on poetic self-pity. '*Friendship causes pain*' is more ammunition for the army of isolationists, but the sentiments are adolescent and barely an improvement on 'Play Me A Sad Song' from eight years before. Even at the time Simon introduced it as, 'Unquestionably my most neurotic song. When I finished it I thought, "Oh man, I can't be this sick!"'

Simon and Garfunkel had been taken on board the rock-and-rollercoaster by this time. In a 1970 *Rolling Stone* interview, Simon recalled a particularly disastrous Simon and Garfunkel gig of the period, arranged to cash in on their chart fame. They had played their latest hit song on a bill with the Four Seasons, the Yardbirds, Mitch Ryder, Chuck Berry and Lou Christie: 'When that was over we said, "we're not ever going to go on stage again; it's ridiculous". . . . So we said, "we'll just make records and that'll be it. Let's go split . . . back to England and really live high". It never stopped after that.'

Mort Lewis, the pair's manager, was an experienced music biz veteran, who steered Simon and Garfunkel in what he considered to be the right direction for those times. He zeroed in on the collegiate audience who were rapidly claiming Simon and Garfunkel as their own, and saw that the duo shunned the package bills they found so unpalatable as well as ignoring the lucrative cabaret circuit. It was in the universities that Simon and Garfunkel, with all those songs about alienation, found an audience who were immediately responsive to them and their music; but they were careful never to over-expose themselves.

A European tour was organized for a fortnight in the late June of 1966, which brought Simon back to the England he had left only a few months before. *Melody Maker*'s Chris Welch interviewed Simon at this time for the paper's 'Pop Think In', where the 'thinker' was asked pertinent questions about himself and contemporary issues. Simon's topics included the predictable Bob Dylan ('the biggest thing Dylan has got going for him is his mystique'); long hair ('I think it's stupid to grow your hair long because its cool . . .') and apartheid ('I think the regime in South Africa is an anachronism . . .'). Simon also underwent *Melody Maker*'s 'Blind Date', where he was played a pile of new singles and tried to guess who they were by. Simon proved that he had a fairly sound knowledge of the contemporary pop scene, although he managed to mistake Otis Redding for both Bobby Vee and Frankie Avalon! He also managed to get in a few digs about Mick Jagger, who seemed for some unknown reason to have incurred his wrath. At one stage he asked Welch: 'What's the truth about Scott Walker and Mick Jagger? Do they really hate each other? Who couldn't hate Mick Jagger?'

Welch spoke to me in 1987 about these interviews: ' "Blind Date" was quite an accolade then. Don't forget this was long before the days of promo videos or TV interviews on *Wogan*; it was one of the few outlets for an articulate pop performer to express himself. He was a prickly character. He seemed almost resentful at having to play the pop media game, although he was very knowledgeable about the whole process. . . . He struck me as someone who was very ambitious and keen to be recognized for his talent. He felt he'd served his apprenticeship and that it was time to move on. There was a kind of arrogance about him, very self-assured, obviously fed up with people comparing his work to Dylan.'

Simon and Garfunkel's 'overnight' arrival at the peak of pop in late 1966 was fortuitous, as rock music was undergoing one of its periodic upheavals which had created something of a vacuum. The Beatles had concluded live performances in August 1966, Dylan was in isolation in Woodstock following his serious motorbike crash in the same month, and the Stones were entering a phase of their career which was to be dogged by repeated drug busts. On the west coast weird bands with even weirder names were beginning to emerge, and on the east coast Andy Warhol's championing of a band called the Velvet Underground was not without interest, but it was a period of change and transition. Pop music was finally becoming an integral part of the new rock culture; and it no longer needed to adhere to, nor had any interest in, the stultifying entertainment industry.

Paul Simon and Art Garfunkel never consciously adapted their material or repertoire to suit the growing underground movement, but their immaculately crafted material continued to find easy refuge on the radio stations. Even parents were already able to recognize a Simon and Garfunkel tune, even if they didn't necessarily agree with or respond to the querulous lyrics. But although their image was refreshingly 'clean cut' for the late 60s, Peter and Gordon they were not! The eminent American music critic Ralph J. Gleason captured the mood of a Simon and Garfunkel concert of the period when he wrote: 'It was starkly simple, almost painfully direct and removed from all showbusiness clichés, with the songs themselves driving deeply and poetically into the very basis of contemporary problems.'

With three hit singles under their belt, Simon and Garfunkel were in the fortunate position of having proved that their success was no mere flash in the pan, that 'The Sounds Of Silence' hadn't been a one-off, and that Simon was more than capable of matching his audience's expectations with a trickle of equally good and frequently better new material. They were now determined to hone their studio expertise and become a substantial addition to the burgeoning rock culture; so, along with the erstwhile Roy Halee, the pair poured everything they had learned during their years together into their fourth single, 'The Dangling Conversation', which was released in September 1966.

'The Dangling Conversation' was a quantum leap for them, bounding far beyond the adolescent angst of 'I Am A Rock'. It was the song that Simon had laboured over longest, and it took the pair more time to record than any previous track. Sadly, that time and trouble was not reflected in the sales figures – the single peaked at Number 25 in America, and totally failed to chart in Britain. It was without doubt Simon's most ambitious song to date, and while such sanctimonious lines as, '*Can analysis be worthwhile/Is the theatre really dead . . .?*' do jar, there is a delicacy and fluency to the song which remains enchanting.

The precision of the arrangement, with its gently plucked guitar, precise use of strings and subdued drum, greatly enhances the song, vividly conveying the '*still life water colour, of the now late afternoon*'. It's a drama played out on the '*borders of our lives*' in that lace-curtained room, where the poetry of Emily Dickinson and Robert Frost is tenderly guarded, not grabbed for protection or a refuge, as in 'I Am A Rock', but is, rather, a life-enhancing comfort. Even the title is evocative – so much of one's formative years seems to be spent in dangling conversations, inconclusive meandering dialogues. I remember how impressed I was with that song on its release. I was at an impressionable age, but then there was a great deal which impressed. As a vivid evocation of sterile relationships and that no-man's-land which has to be crossed in order to move on and mature, it marked the beginning of a new facet of Simon's writing. He was at last dealing with recognizable situations and circumstances, but couched in terms and using structures which were undeniably the work of a maturing writer.

As a taster for their forthcoming album, this single was a beguiling introduction. *Parsley, Sage, Rosemary and Thyme* was released in November 1966, but while it was a marked improvement on the two earlier Simon and Garfunkel albums, it still showed an uncomfortable reliance on songs which Simon had written years before. There was 'Big Bright Green Pleasure Machine' which Simon had written in an all-night launderette near Judith Piepe's flat, and which proved to be an outsider's jaundiced view of the topical hippie movement, with an astute line that bored close to the heart of the problem: '*Do you sleep alone when others sleep in pairs?*' 'A Poem On The Underground Wall' dated from the same period and concerned Simon's observations of tube travelling, coming from gigs around London to the East End. 'A Simple Desultory Philippic' was an updated version of the song which had appeared the year before on the *Songbook*, while both 'Patterns' and 'Flowers Never Bend With The Rainfall' also dated from Simon's days in England, and had appeared as solo versions on *Songbook*. Even 'Feelin' Groovy', that archetypal New York song, had its genesis in London – Judith Piepe can remember Simon's delight at having written such a happy song for a change.

The album's title comes from the refrain of 'Scarborough Fair', and in his notes to the song on his own album, Martin Carthy wrote: 'The herbs mentioned (parsley, sage, rosemary and thyme) are all known to have been closely associated with death and also as charms against the evil eye.' But even this traditional song, in

Simon's hands, borrowed from his earlier work, incorporating segments from 'The Side Of A Hill'.

Garfunkel was given full range on the lush 'For Emily, Whenever I May Find Her' (Emily Dickinson again?). He manages to make words such as organdie, crinoline and juniper mesh into the full sweep of the song, which gave him ample opportunity to demonstrate the magnificent range of his voice. Of the 'up' songs, 'The 59th Street Bridge Song (Feelin' Groovy)' perfectly captures that *'dappled and drowsy'* early morning feeling, content and happily relaxed, but not tired enough to sleep. Typically though, Simon felt that 'Feelin' Groovy' was altogether too frivolous a title, even given the inherent frivolity of the song; now it was to be enshrined on vinyl he insisted on preceding it with the more pretentious 'The 59th Street Bridge Song'. The song's accompaniment featured two members of jazzman Dave Brubeck's old group, and was indicative of Simon and Garfunkel's desire to extend their sound, noticeable on the string arrangement of 'The Dangling Conversation' and the aural montage of '7 O'Clock News/Silent Night'.

'Cloudy' gives an interesting insight into Simon's cultural parameters of the period: *'From Tolstoy to Tinkerbell'*, from Russia's finest novelist to the whimsical sprite of J. M. Barrie's *Peter Pan*. 'A Simple Desultory Philippic' had appeared on the *Songbook*, but here Simon had added a few more jive references, including yet another put-down of Dylan: at the song's conclusion, you can hear a clunk and Simon whinging 'I've lost my harmonica Albert' – Dylan's then manager was one Albert Grossman. Lenny Bruce also crops up on the song, and his death from a drug overdose (in August 1966) is mentioned on the '7 O'Clock News' segment of 'Silent Night' which closes the album. In America, the album was dedicated to Bruce's memory; both Simon and Garfunkel were admirers and had witnessed his classic Village performances before narcotics and law suits sapped his vitality.

One of Simon's most underrated songs is 'A Poem On The Underground Wall' which is driven by a breakneck bass and guitar riff. The man who writes *that* four letter word on the wall is no prophet, it's a gesture that his 'most peculiar man' might have made as a final stab at immortality before his lonely death. In Simon's hands the word, *'slashed deep upon the advertising'*, is not mindless graffiti, but a desperate plea to be heard from a man alienated by the society which surrounds him. With such paeans to the outsider, and his obvious sympathy for underdogs, Simon was attracting quite a reputation as an expert in alienation. He told Jon Landau in a

Rolling Stone interview of 1972: 'Everybody says, "You seem to write a lot about alienation . . . alienation seems to be your big theme". "That's my theme", I said, and proceeded to write more about alienation.'

On songs like 'The Dangling Conversation', though, Simon was clearly growing in another direction, even if he himself dismissed it as 'English major stuff'. Already you could sense Simon's reluctance to be just another pop songwriter; although he resented the praise lavished on such rock poets as Dylan and John Lennon; they were an élite which Simon wished himself a part of. He told Robert Shelton of the *New York Times* in 1966: 'Pop music has become the most exciting area of all music today', but later in the same interview acknowledged its limitations and spoke of wishing to expand into areas beyond the three-minute pop song, like the novel. He had spoken of these ambitions as early as 1965 when he told Alan Smith of the *New Musical Express*: 'I'm attacking it by doing short stories . . . developing character studies. . . . I'm treating these themes that I treat often. . . . Isolation. Loneliness. Communication. By developing these character studies I'll incorporate them eventually into this novel.'

Twenty years on, the Paul Simon novel remains unrealized. He had a short prose piece 'On Drums And Other Hollow Songbooks' published around this time, and of course tackled the screenplay for his film *One Trick Pony* in the late 70s, but the ability comfortably to master prose was a skill which eluded Simon. As recently as 1986, talking about the sleeve notes on *Graceland*, Simon admitted: 'My prose style is pretty much as it was in college.'

The most mature work on *Parsley, Sage, Rosemary and Thyme* – the last album of new material for nearly two years – displayed Simon's confidence in his ability as a songwriter. People were beginning to notice the quality of his songs, and the scrupulous attention to detail Simon, Garfunkel and Halee paid to their recordings. Simon admitted that 'The Dangling Conversation' was vaguely influenced by T. S. Eliot and also wryly noted that it wasn't that his lyrics were that good, it was just that everyone else's at the time were so bad! The consistency of Simon's lyrics over the years has gone largely unremarked; but he did undeniably bring a much-needed poetic discipline to the largely haphazard rock music format. His eye for detail was acute and his willingness to experiment with blank verse and fractured song structures marked him out as an innovator.

Simon and Garfunkel (and manager Lewis) had identified their core audience early on; Simon primly informed *Record Mirror* in

1966: 'The college audience is ideal for us. . . . We can talk to the audience and communicate. You see, although teenage pop kids buy my records, I find it a little hard to communicate with them. We don't have that much in common.' Again there is that tone of arrogance which Simon's contemporaries on the English folk scene had already noted. Even when popular success eluded him, Simon obviously had an unshakably high opinion of himself and his work. He railed at *Record Mirror*'s Norman Jopling during a 1967 British tour: 'The Seekers and the Bachelors. . . . What kind of an image are we getting with our songs being recorded by groups like that? Our version of "The Sounds of Silence" was far superior to the Bachelors'. . . . Take "The Dangling Conversation", it just wasn't suitable for the British market, it was above the kids.' Of 'The 59th Street Bridge Song', Simon immodestly told Jopling: 'I knew that record was a hit as soon as I wrote it.' Strangely though, the song wasn't a hit in America for Simon and Garfunkel, but for Harper's Bizarre who covered the song, a version of which Simon was characteristically uncomplimentary.

Simon may have had a point – 'The Dangling Conversation' *was* undoubtedly his finest song to date and deserved to be a hit – but remarks like those won him few new friends. No audience likes to be told that they are stupid and unable to appreciate merit, or that certain songs are 'above them'. No one denies an artist the right to believe in his own ability, but to be scorned by that artist for lack of discernment is unpalatable. Presumably Simon's distaste for cover versions didn't stop him collecting hefty royalty cheques.

Without doubt, audiences were changing. Rock and roll had always been aimed primarily at a teenage audience, and as that audience grew older it was replaced by a new avaricious young crowd, eager for their own idols. By the end of 1966, the Beatles and their teenage fans, who had worshipped the idea of the Fab Four, were growing up; to fill that gap and keep the lucrative teenage pop audience satisfied, the Monkees were created.

Rock music, though, was gravitating towards albums as a means of expressing ideas and exploring philosophies which the single denied. It was now an integral part of an alternative culture which catered for young adults. The first full flowering of these tribes was in January 1967 at San Francisco's Human 'Be-In'; but the event which came to be regarded as the time it all came together, during that hectic Summer of Love, was the first Monterey International Pop Festival in June 1967.

Feelin' Groovy

> Adolescents drifted from city to torn city, sloughing both the past and the future as snakes shed their skins, children who were never taught and would now never learn the games that held the society together. People were missing. Children were missing. Parents were missing. Those left behind left desultory missing persons reports, then moved on themselves.

So wrote Joan Didion in her essay of the time, 'Slouching Towards Bethlehem'. It was a period when all roads led to San Francisco (where, of course, it was de rigueur to wear some flowers in your hair). Jann Wenner, on his way to founding *Rolling Stone*, wrote of Monterey: 'It was a superb moment for rock and roll – an example of the style for which Californian music has become famous. This is the first music festival of its kind, and the first to be run by the artists themselves and was a general success. The star of the show was San Francisco and the sound of that city.' Clive Davis from CBS called Monterey 'a glimpse of the new world'. It was a cynosure for all the optimists, who by then believed that rock and roll could be a powerful and unique force for good.

In April 1967, Paul Simon was asked to be on the steering committee of directors for the Monterey Festival, along with the Mamas and the Papas' John Phillips, Paul McCartney, Brian Wilson and Mick Jagger. The directors co-ordinated the roster of artists and were also asked to suggest where any money raised might go; Simon suggested New York singer-songwriter Laura Nyro as an addition to the bill, and ensured that $50,000 was earmarked for guitar workshops in Harlem. In his autobiography, *Papa John*, Phillips recalls Simon at the festival kidding him that with his success with the Mamas and the Papas he had sold out, and laconically maintaining that he and Artie were 'out of England. We're folk. We're pure!'

For all the peace and love vibes at Monterey that weekend in June

1967, there were warring factions, primarily those of the San Francisco housebands like the Grateful Dead and Jefferson Airplane, who were keen to keep the plastic showbiz bands of LA away from Monterey. As a 'neutral New Yorker', Simon was asked to act as a go-between. This entailed a trip to the Grateful Dead mansion on Haight Street, which he called 'the spookiest place I've ever seen', but his negotiations were successful, the festival went ahead, and San Francisco became synonymous with a new beginning. The city's graceful, Gothic architecture, its benign tolerance of artistic communities, its sanctioning of Bohemia, ensured that it became both the centre and symbol of the 1967 Summer of Love.

Monterey marked the only festival appearance of Simon and Garfunkel, where they closed the bill on the opening Friday night. As the fog rolled in and swathed the festival site, they played an enchanting set, which included the première of 'Punky's Dilemma', and held the audience spellbound. Just two voices and a guitar, they were a stark and moving contrast to the pyrotechnics of The Who and Jimi Hendrix. D. A. Pennebaker, whose documentary, *Monterey Pop*, vividly captured the event, remembered Simon and Garfunkel's contribution for me in London in 1987: 'A watershed? I felt a little water coming over the shed, yes. I guess I had some sense of it, it was impossible not to . . . I had a sense about what I thought it should be about, but I really wasn't prepared for the excitement. It was history. A kind of popular history. I think then, for the first time, people considered that that kind of history was relevant; up until then you were supposed to study presidents and generals, and suddenly this was as good a thing to remember as anything else . . . Paul had some long ten-minute thing he wanted in the film, but their "59th Street Bridge Song" was exactly what the film needed. It seemed to capture the atmosphere of the event, it's exactly the sort of song the film needed because no one else can sing that kind of song.'

In hindsight, Monterey was undoubtedly a watershed. Local bands like the Grateful Dead, Jefferson Airplane, Country Joe and the Fish and Janis Joplin reached a wider audience and went on to nationwide acclaim. The audience was also alerted to the huge diversity of music being nurtured by the love generation, the spellbinding sitar of Ravi Shankar, the gut-wrenching soul of Otis Redding, the cool blue jazz of Hugh Masekela. For all its hippy-dippy idealism married to hard-headed business, Monterey was a triumph. It was an artistic melting pot. Brian Jones could wander unhindered amongst the crowd, Monkee Peter Tork and

Above left: Crew Cut Kids: Tom (Arthur Garfunkel) and Jerry (Paul Simon) in 1957; promotional shot for 'Hey Schoolgirl'. (*Michael Ochs Archives*)

Above right: So Young And Yet So Full Of Pain: Simon and Garfunkel together in New York just after 'The Sounds Of Silence' hit in early 1966. (*Michael Ochs Archives*)

Below: Rare shot of three of pop music's most successful songwriters together in the early Sixties – Carole King, Paul Simon and Gerry Goffin. (*Michael Ochs Archives*)

Paul Simon gives sessionman Al Kooper the finger in 1966. (*Michael Ochs Archives*)

The Caped Crusader and friend, on the road again, 1966. (*David Redfern*)

Paul Simon in 1966 enjoying his second stab at success – RIP Tom and Jerry, The Lone Teen-Ranger, Jerry Landis and Paul Kane. (*Rex Features*)

Simon and Garfunkel share a dangling conversation at TV rehearsal in 1967. (*David Redfern*)

A pensive Paul Simon in 1969 just after the release of 'The Boxer'. (*Michael Ochs Archives*)

The Poet and One-Man-Band – Paul Simon in 1973. (*Michael Ochs Archives*)

George Harrison and Paul Simon together on TV's *Saturday Night Live* in 1975. (*London Features International*)

Jonah Levin (Paul Simon) attempts reconciliation with wife Marion (Blair Brown) in 1980's *One-Trick Pony*. (*Kobal Collection*)

Together again: Simon and Garfunkel after European press conference to announce their 1982 reunion tour. (*Stills/Rex Features*)

Simon and Garfunkel at rehearsal for American date on their contentious 1982 tour. (*Janet Macoska/Retna*)

Above: Paul Simon (*bottom left*) at historic recording of USA For Africa's 'We Are The World', January 1985. (*Kobal Collection*)

Right: Paul Simon in London, August 1986, after *Graceland* press conference. (*Stills/Rex Features*)

Below: Brothers in arms: (*l. to r.*) Mark Knopfler, Paul Simon, Peter Gabriel and Eric Clapton together after sweeping the board at the 1987 BPI awards in London. (*Phil Loftus/L.F.I.*)

The 'other' Paul Simon, actor Chevy Chase, joins the real thing on stage at Madison Square Garden, New York, in 1987 to recreate the 'You Can Call Me Al' video. (*Nick Elgar/L.F.I.*)

Paul Simon and his second wife, actress and author Carrie Fisher. (*Janet Macoska/Retna*)

Above left: For Simon, the most enjoyable aspect of the *Graceland* project was the opportunity to work with Ladysmith Black Mambazo's Joseph Shabalala; the two are pictured together soon after the album's release. (*Phil Loftus/L.F.I.*)

Above right: (l. to r.) Miriam Makeba, Ray Phiri, Paul Simon and Hugh Masekela pictured together outside London's ICA in February 1987. (*Clive Dixon/Rex Features*)

Below: Every generation throws a hero up the pop charts: Paul Simon soon after the release of the multi-million selling *Graceland* in 1986. (*Michael Putland/Retna*)

Left: Paul Simon joined on stage by Ladysmith Black Mambazo to perform the unforgettable 'Diamonds On The Soles Of Her Shoes', 1987. (*David Redfern*)

Right: The man at the eye of the *Graceland* hurricane, Paul Simon, on stage performing 'The Boxer', his only solo song of the show. (*David Redfern*)

Left: The moving climax of the *Graceland* shows: the entire troupe gathered to sing the ANC anthem 'N'Kosi Sikeleli' which ended every show on the tour during 1987. (*David Redfern*)

Paul Simon could swap licks on guitar, Simon even got to jam with Jimi Hendrix, but was wisely content to play rhythm to Hendrix's blistering lead. Simon called the event 'a jubilee'. That sense of innocence, openness and discovery would sadly never be recaptured. With Woodstock in 1969 as its apotheosis, Altamont five months later was the festival nemesis.

Sgt. Pepper's Lonely Hearts Club Band was released a fortnight before Monterey, and 1967 looked set to be Year One of the new culture. It was also the year that debut albums from promising new names like David Bowie, Traffic, Jimi Hendrix, the Doors and the Velvet Underground were released. Hailed as pop music's finest hour on its release, *Sgt. Pepper* led rock music on a wild goose chase down a blind alley. Everyone felt they had to match up to the Beatles, and rock's arteries were clogged for far too long with elaborate, mind-blowing concept albums, with plenty of space on the sleeve for suitably psychedelic lyrics.

The worthlessness of 'The Sons of Pepper' was soon manifest; Paul Simon was too wily a writer to fall into that trap, but Simon and Garfunkel's first single of that transcendental year could not but help observe the changes. 'At The Zoo' was ostensibly a New York song, but managed to combine some of the west coast exhilaration with Simon's native east coast scepticism. The human zoo in the final verse contains all the stereotypes which make up society, with the hamsters at the song's conclusion *'turning on'*. *'What a gas!'* enthuses Simon, *'You gotta come and see, at the zoo'*. 'Fakin' It', the duo's second single of the year, would crop up again on *Bookends* the following year, but the B side is the otherwise unobtainable 'You Don't Know Where Your Interest Lies'. Today, Simon's lyrics would arouse the wrath of feminists; early on he blithely informs us that he is *'womanly wise'*, and tells the woman in the song, the object of his scorn, *'you're just a game that I like to play'*.

'A Hazy Shade Of Winter', released as a single in late 1966, found Simon poring over *'manuscripts of unpublished rhyme'*, and it was that reluctance to publish which led to problems over Simon and Garfunkel's next major project, the scoring of the 1967 film *The Graduate*.

One durable aspect of the counter culture proved to be its unabashed challenging of established ideas. The American Dream had been found wanting, there had to be an alternative to the two-child, two-car, two-parent nuclear family. The hippies challenged that establishment in many ways, and predictably the entertainment industry endorsed that challenge, sensing further fields of profit in their affront. It was to be a further two years before Dennis Hopper and Peter Fonda's genuinely alternative *Easy Rider* would success-fully loosen the Hollywood stranglehold. But a notable first step was taken in Mike Nichols' film of *The Graduate*.

When the novel on which the film was based was first published in 1963, it attracted encouraging reviews and favourable compari-sons to J. D. Salinger's *Catcher In The Rye*, which had so epitomized the nascent rebellion of the 50s. Charles Webb's novel delineated the dissatisfaction of one Benjamin Braddock – recent college graduate – who rejected the empty values of his parents, while failing to replace them with any of his own. Significantly, the film's final scene, where Benjamin and his true love Elaine drive off in the bus, shows neither of them speaking to each other, already well on their way to becoming the very sort of parents they so despise.

The film's director Mike Nichols had been lured to Hollywood in 1966 after a glistening career as a Broadway director. Prior to that, he and Elaine May had been the leading satirists of their generation, and their years together between 1957 and 1961 had been characterized by shows of acerbic wit and potent satire. Nichols' Hollywood debut had been an acclaimed version of Edward Albee's coruscating *Who's Afraid Of Virginia Woolf?*, which had won Elizabeth Taylor her second Oscar. As far as Hollywood was concerned, the thirty-five-year-old Nichols was hot. After much soul-searching, Nichols selected the then un-known Dustin Hoffman to play the maladroit Benjamin, and he engaged the laconic Buck Henry to fashion a screenplay out of Webb's novel. The casting of the seductive Mrs Robinson was also crucial; eventually Anne Bancroft became the older woman fantasy of a generation – but only after Doris Day had declined the role!

Nichols was familiar with his younger brother's copy of the *Parsley, Sage, Rosemary and Thyme* album, and approached Paul Simon with a view to creating a score for his forthcoming film. Hindsight reveals it to have been a masterstroke; Simon's score allied to Henry's brilliantly witty script and Hoffman's definitive performance saw *The Graduate* ensconced as one of the key films of the 60s, and one of the first authentic 'rock' films.

In these days when films seem to be concocted solely to provide a spin-off soundtrack album (*Top Gun, Iron Eagle*), it is hard to remember just how significant a breakthrough *The Graduate* was. Prior to that, pop films were rarely little more than cash-ins – take the money and run vehicles for stars whose fifteen minutes of fame had to be capitalized on before the next idol was thrown up. Elvis' initial films had shown some promise, but throughout the 60s he had become enmeshed in a series of films which set new lows even for Hollywood. As with so many other facets of entertainment, it was the Beatles who broke the mould, notably in the quasi-documentary *A Hard Day's Night* (1964), although the following year *Help!* had subsided into a psychedelic farrago, with Lennon moaning that they were guest stars in their own film. There had been successful theme songs to films prior to *The Graduate*, but no mainstream Hollywood film had ever before attempted to integrate a rock score onto film, with the songs providing a subtext of the character's innermost thoughts, thus saving on pages of dialogue, and establishing scene and character in a less obtrusive way and with a modicum of effort.

Simon was flattered that Mike Nichols should approach him. He had a high regard for Nichols' work with Elaine May and, despite considering the novel to be 'bad Salinger', relished the opportunity of scoring a film. However, it was not long before he became disillusioned with the primitive machinery and disinterested crafts-men prevalent in film studios. He realized how much happier he was creating his own music in tandem with Garfunkel and Halee on the best studio equipment CBS could offer.

The two songs Simon eventually submitted for the film – 'Overs' and 'Punky's Dilemma' – were rejected by Nichols. With deadlines going crazy, Nichols, in desperation, started using extant Simon and Garfunkel songs to accompany sequences as they were completed, simply as a stopgap guideline until Simon found his muse and was inspired to pen new material. But as time went by, fresh material was still not forthcoming, and the more he saw the rushes with the temporary Simon and Garfunkel songs in place, the more Nichols became convinced that the existing songs – 'The Sounds of Silence', 'The Big Bright Green Pleasure Machine', 'Scarborough Fair' and 'April Come She Will' – were ideal.

The song which became indelibly linked with *The Graduate* was 'Mrs Robinson', which is surprisingly never heard in full on the soundtrack album or in the film. Simon had been playing around with the melody and a vague idea of the mood of the lyrics for some time, but needed a three-syllable name to slot in to the song which was provisionally known as 'Mrs Roosevelt'. Eventually, though loath to write to order, Simon and Garfunkel began to fashion the song around the Anne Bancroft character. On learning of the song's existence Nichols immediately requested a performance and subsequently demanded that Simon concentrate his energies on finishing the song.

Simon did eventually finish 'Mrs Robinson' which went on to become Simon and Garfunkel's best-selling single to date and wound up on their own *Bookends* album in 1968. But in the film, 'Mrs Robinson' is heard only as an instrumental and in a shortened version with altered lyrics: '*Stand up tall, Mrs Robinson/God in Heaven smiles on those who pray/Hey, hey, hey*'. The song is most memorably used near the film's climax as Benjamin rushes to the church to thwart Elaine's wedding . . . the riff slows down on Simon's guitar just as Benjamin's car runs out of petrol.

On its release, the film was hailed as 'a milestone of American cinema', and the *New York Times* even carried a twenty-six page article dissecting and analysing the reason's for its success. But the thorny question of the soundtrack album had still to be resolved. . . .

Clive Davis at CBS had firsthand experience of how valuable a commodity soundtrack albums could be. They had provided his label with many of its main successes in the late 50s and early 60s. Like everyone else in the music business, Davis looked with envy at *The Sound of Music* soundtrack which had dominated the album charts for months following the film's release in 1965. When he learnt that one of his acts had been approached to supply the soundtrack for a film which insiders had already tipped as an off the wall smash, Davis was delighted and sat back expecting it to be an extremely profitable undertaking for his company.

Naturally Davis had assumed that having agreed to write the soundtrack for the film, Simon would come up with a batch of new songs, but Simon and Garfunkel, preoccupied with their follow up to *Parsley, Sage, Rosemary and Thyme*, had spent much of 1967 in the studio creating what eventually became *Bookends*. The consequent absence of new songs in the film created huge problems for CBS' planned release of a soundtrack album.

Simon and Garfunkel and their manager Mort Lewis felt strongly that fans could not be palmed off with an album of material all of which was already available on their previous albums, and which anyway only totalled a meagre fifteen minutes. Davis was stunned, but still convinced that *The Graduate* could propel Simon and Garfunkel into the higher reaches of superstardom. On seeing the finished film, Davis noticed Dave Grusin's additional music – hot little numbers like 'The Singleman Party Foxtrot' and 'Sun Porch Cha Cha Cha' – and went back suggesting that the Simon and

Garfunkel songs could be bolstered by Grusin's music. He thought this could be the formula for a successful soundtrack album. But Simon was not impressed and told Davis: 'We've been working on the *Bookends* album a long time, we love it, and we think it's a major creative breakthrough. We don't want to wait six months to release it just because of your commercial problems.' But while Davis respected Simon and Garfunkel's artistic impulses, he was also an astute judge of the market-place, and insisted that *The Graduate* should surface as an album in its own right. The way he saw it, *Bookends* could be released simultaneously for established fans who would welcome the new songs, while recent converts fired by the movie could use the soundtrack album as an introduction. Finally, reluctantly, Simon and Garfunkel agreed and were more than a little surprised to see *The Graduate* become a huge commercial success.

The film hit a nerve and it went on to become one of the box office giants of the 60s. In that year's Oscars, Mike Nichols won the Best Director statue, but Simon's music was ignored. The 1967 award for Best Original Song went to 'Talk To The Animals' from *Dr Dolittle*, while Best Original Score was *Thoroughly Modern Millie*! But some consolation was forthcoming when, half-way through 1968, *The Graduate* was the Number 1 album in America, 'Mrs Robinson' was comfortably at the top of the singles charts, and the new Simon and Garfunkel album wasn't far behind.

The turbulence of 1968 in America was unparalleled: a haggard Lyndon Johnson, brought down by the Vietnam war, appeared on TV to say he would not seek re-election; Martin Luther King and Robert Kennedy fell victim to assassins' bullets; the Vietcong launched the Tet offensive, which proved they were a viable fighting force, and that the US had no chance of beating such committed troops. Drugs were playing a major role in distancing children from their parents, while Vietnam hung like a sword of Damocles over the land of the brave and the home of the free.

With the country in turmoil, and a presidential election looming, the youth of America, for one brief, shining moment, did seem united behind candidate Eugene McCarthy, a Democrat running on a Stop The War Ticket. Along with Creedence Clearwater Revival, then just getting into their stride, Simon and Garfunkel, Janis Joplin and John Sebastian played a McCarthy benefit at Shea Stadium, which helped raise around $100,000 for his campaign. But even the might of the contemporary rock world couldn't stop Richard M. Nixon sweeping into office in November 1968.

Bookends had its finger on the turbulent pulse of America during 1968. The peace and love vibes from San Francisco had found themselves replaced by militancy. In Europe, students took to the streets to protest over the growing US involvement in Vietnam, and back in the States students were burning their draft cards rather than go and fight in a war that none believed in. But the establishment, in the shape of Nixon's repressive government, would soon be cracking down. At the Democratic Convention in Chicago, Mayor Daley's police had literally run riot; and the older generation, so vilified the year before, were turning their thoughts to keeping their young in line.

Bookends was the result of obsessive care in the studio. Simon and Garfunkel tested the CBS studios to the full, linking up two eight-track machines and using them simultaneously to give a sixteen-track effect; they were determined to achieve a scrupulously pristine sound in their recordings, regardless of how long it took. As Judith Piepe so acutely observed of the album, years later, 'It was the first time that Paul could use the studio like a guitar.'

Simon and Garfunkel, together with Roy Halee (who was by now an *éminence grise* to the duo in the same way that George Martin was to the Beatles), had spent months slaving over the album and it remains their finest vinyl testament. But even *Bookends* suffered from Simon's lack of prolificity as a writer – side two only featured one new song, 'Punky's Dilemma', the rest of the songs having previously been released as singles. 'Fakin' It' was one of these: it originated in a 'hashish reverie' during which Simon speculated on his earlier incarnation as a Jewish tailor in the middle Europe of the nineteenth century. Trivia fans may be interested to learn that the Mr Leitch mentioned in the lyrics is Donovan, while the welcoming girl was Beverley, John Martyn's wife and acquaintance of Simon's in his London days. 'Punky's Dilemma' was Simon's caustic east coast view of the vagaries of the west coast; you could just imagine a movement out there, with proto-Yuppies sporting their 'Citizens For Boysenberry Jam' badges!

The previous year *Sgt. Pepper* had paved the way for innumerable derivative concept albums (*In-A-Gadda-Da-Vida* anyone?), but Simon and Garfunkel's *Bookends* perhaps comes closest to equalling that ambitious concept. Side one of the album is a suite which traces a character from birth to lonely death. From the gentle, solitary 'birth' plucked out by Simon on acoustic guitar, it crackles with the fuzzy bass explosion which ushers in 'Save The Life of My Child', a classic cinema vignette-style song. The serenity of its acoustic opening is deceptive. 'Save The Life of My Child' plunges the listener into the chaos of America in 1968: the kids high on drugs, disrespectful of figures in authority. ('What's become of the children?' was the question which echoed round the nation that year.) The multi-tracked vocals are phased and given an eerie presence of their own, like faces freed from the personal hell of a Francis Bacon painting. Buried in the final mix Simon and Garfunkel can be heard singing the opening lines of 'The Sounds of Silence', a dig at the CBS reworking of the song; a technique Paul McCartney had used the previous year when, during the fade of the Beatles' 'All You Need Is Love', he can be heard singing a discordant snatch of 'She Loves You' – both Simon and McCartney enjoyed mocking their earlier existences.

The chaos and craziness of youth on the album's first song are replaced by the wistful developing relationship in 'America'. It has become one of Simon's most popular songs, ironic considering it is so much a song of its time and that it is in blank verse, a rare feat for a popular song. Surely part of the reason for the song's enduring appeal is again in Simon's cinematic style of writing: a dreamy camera following the star-crossed lovers on a Greyhound odyssey to find the real America, and themselves into the bargain. Voyages of discovery were very much a feature of the late 60s, when dissent began to be replaced by a search for the fundamental values and strengths of an earlier, more innocent America (a theme which also occupied Simon in the final verse of 'Mrs Robinson'). The Kathy of 'Homeward Bound' is here a companion on the voyage, and Simon's pithy lyrics and exact ear for conversation lend the song a degree of authenticity few can match. The language of lovers is so perfectly observed, with private jokes and face-spotting other passengers, the lack of cigarettes, reading magazines, while in a beautiful image of movement and distance '*the moon rose over an open field*'.

The song's climax sheds light on the universal quest, but as in the final scene of *The Graduate*, the individuals' inability to communicate is tragically apparent. The song's narrator is '*empty and aching*' without knowing why; something has gone sourly wrong with himself and his country, and in a vision of a suburban Armageddon he imagines the New Jersey turnpike clogged with cars all keen to search for their own vision of an America that has gone, perhaps forever. The turnpike was where Jack Kerouac began his odysseys on the road in the 50s; it's a place for beginnings, but also a place where journeys come to their own sad, solitary ends.

Ten years on, the lovers' sense of exploration and discovery has been replaced by weary confinement at the stale conclusion of their marriage. 'Overs' begins with a cigarette lit (although *ZigZag* reasoned it must be a joint) and Simon carefully, precisely, delineates a failed and bitter marriage, with *'no times at all except the* New York Times!' The song's most telling line is the bitter *'We're just a habit like saccharin'*. The lack of lavish production echoes the sparseness of feeling within the relationship, like the barren emptiness of a Beckett play. The final verse reveals the narrator's weakness; he is unable to break out of the stale farce his marriage has become. Each time one partner tries to leave, they stop and think it over, and in that pause for consideration lie the seeds of their doom. Each pause merely reinforces their failure and their inability actually to do anything about it. They will carry on together, and their sentence will never be commuted.

'Voices Of Old People' is Garfunkel's most obvious contribution to the suite, and its weakest point, a bone that sticks in the throat of an otherwise flawless suite. Touching as the voices are, all the sad resignation of old age eroding their lives and forcing them to face the futility of those lives jars in the otherwise seamless structure of Simon's songs.

The collection is beautifully concluded with 'Old Friends'. Beginning gently with the vivid image of two old men, seated alone together *'like bookends'*, the song progresses – with the help of Jimmy Haskell's striking string arrangement – through a series of graphic, precise images (the city's noises 'sift' through to the park, the round-toed old men are 'lost' in their overcoats . . .). Through an orchestral reprise of the 'Bookends' theme developed from Simon's solo introduction, the song arrives wearily, resignedly at its conclusion: *'How terribly strange to be seventy'*. A small but perceptive point from a writer of twenty-seven: the *strangeness* of old age. The Rolling Stones sneered *'What a drag it is getting old'*, The Who's nihilism begged to die before they got old; Simon accepts that he too will grow old, but is unsure how he will be able to cope with his arrival at that terminus. It is that sense of awareness which concludes the suite with the lovely, lilting threnody as Simon and Garfunkel sing, *'Time it was, and what a time it was . . .'*. Simon concludes that the only succour for your dotage is your memories; love, time, success will all have run out, but your memories will be a companion. At the end, that's all you're left with, a head full of memories, and a faded sepia photograph of how it once was. Like the photograph on the cover of *Bookends*: two young men at the peak of their creativity and success, their eyes locked on Richard Avedon's camera, almost translucent, like star children from Kubrick's *2001: A Space Odyssey*, which was the cinematic talking point of that year.

Financially *The Graduate* had propelled Simon and Garfunkel to the top, artistically *Bookends* saw the pair installed as part of the rock elite. Two years after their first Number 1 single, Simon and Garfunkel were back at the top with 'Mrs Robinson'. People still puzzle over the song's relevance to the Anne Bancroft character from the movie; a reasoned guess, however, is that the song follows on from her state at the film's conclusion, and finds her safely sedated in an institution to recover from the shame. To be humiliated before your friends precipitates a breakdown, and '*most of all, you've got to hide it from the kids*'. But the last verse saw the song broaden in its ambition, with Simon conjuring up a vision of the lost innocence of America and its hunger for contemporary heroes. The line '*Where have you gone Joe DiMaggio/A nation turns its lonely eyes to you?*' begs the question of where America could look for heroes during that confused and convulsive summer of 1968 when the best and brightest were struck down by bullets and clubs. DiMaggio was America's last hero. The nation's greatest ball player had effected a marriage made in Heaven when he married Marilyn Monroe after his retirement, and he remained a potent symbol well into the 1980s, when the Ball Player in Nic Roeg's film *Insignificance* was obviously modelled on DiMaggio.

But '*Joltin' Joe has left and gone away*', and the young were left confusingly searching for substitute father figures with which to identify. Simon was justifiably proud of the song, pleased that he had managed to use the word Jesus in a non-religious popular song, though sad he couldn't work in the name of the Yankees star hitter Mickey Mantle; he told Mantle it was nothing personal, 'just a matter of syllables!' The single won Simon and Garfunkel two Grammys in 1968, and the Grammy for Best Original Score Written for a Motion Picture went to Simon for *The Graduate*, although Simon himself thought 'Hey Jude' would have sewn up the Grammys that year. Mrs Robinson's refrain 'Coo coo ca choo' owed a nod to Lennon's 'I Am The Walrus', but also reminded any remaining Tom and Jerry fans of the chorus of 'Hey Schoolgirl'. It was to become one of Simon's most covered songs; Frank Sinatra gave it a horrendous overkill treatment, while one of Simon's preferred versions was Booker T and The MG's 'very funky' treatment.

Predictably, after the success of *The Graduate*, Simon was inundated with requests to write film scores; he wisely turned down Franco Zeffirelli's film biography of St Francis of Assisi, *Brother Sun and Sister Moon*, and rashly declined to undertake the score for *Midnight Cowboy*, justifying his refusal with the laconic comment: 'I didn't want to look like Dustin Hoffman's song-writer.' In fact *Midnight Cowboy*'s influence could be detected on the *Bridge Over Troubled Water* album; the back cover shot is a dead ringer of a Hoffman/Jon Voight pose from the film, and in 'Keep The Customer Satisfied', Simon is determined to '*keep one step ahead of the shoeshine*' – in the film Ratso's father was a bootblack.

Manfred Mann had a hit in 1968 with the engaging 'My Name Is Jack', written by one John Simon, who many rumoured was in fact Paul Simon. There are elements of Simon's writing style in the song, notably the line '*The Greta Garbo Home for wayward boys and girls*', but there really was a John Simon and he had in fact co-produced a number of songs on *Bookends*! Our Mr Simon made one of his rare guest appearances on an album when, in 1968, he appeared on the double album, *The Live Adventures Of Al Kooper and Mike Bloomfield*; the two former Dylan sidemen had recorded a slow, bluesy version of 'Feelin' Groovy' which Simon enjoyed, and he went into the studio to add his own harmonies.

Paul Simon could look back on 1968 with due cause for satisfaction. His own dissatisfaction with Simon and Garfunkel's output in late 1966 and early 1967 had been overcome and he had achieved an artistic triumph with side one of *Bookends*. *The Graduate* had helped the duo break through to a massive new audience and 'Mrs Robinson' had been showered with the sort of accolades that made Simon and Garfunkel members of the rock aristocracy.

Al Stewart gave me a picture of Paul Simon during that hectic year, the last time he saw Paul: 'In 1968, on my first trip to New York, I crashed a party in the Village. I had nowhere to stay, but met a girl called Enid who let me crash on her couch. I found Paul's number and left a message with his answering service. At 3 a.m. I was sitting round watching TV, the phone rings and Enid – who was pretty pissed off I was still around – came in, a changed woman, "Do you know Paul Simon? *The* Paul Simon? He's on the phone asking for you!" Paul told me they were playing Cornell the next day, and asked "Do you want to be a roadie for the day?" I should have learned – Paul never paid me for the Jackson C. Frank session, but I thought what the hell. Anyway, the Rolls turned up outside Enid's place, which was in a pretty run down neighbourhood, with Artie, Paul and Mort. *The Graduate* had just been released and they were superstars. I carried the guitars for the gig and on the way back we stopped off at a fast food joint for a burger, and there was absolute pandemonium at the sight of Simon and Garfunkel getting a burger. The owner rushed us all into a back room, but some big Jewish mother figure rushed up and embraced Paul and said, "You're just the sort of boy I'd want my daughter to marry!" '

With a Number 1 single and albums, the interest in Simon and Garfunkel's back catalogue had been reawakened, and at one stage during the year they had the top three albums in the American charts. Appropriately a hit single of that summer by the 1910 Fruitgum Co. was called 'Simon Says'. By the end of 1968, Simon and Garfunkel were not only the most successful act on the CBS roster, but the most popular group in America. The relationship between Paul and Artie was strong, buoyed by their success; the two drew on their long friendship together to tide them over the assault of fame and its inherent pressures. In 1983 Simon described the period as 'Great . . . the best time ever. The hits just kept rolling in'.

The boy in the bubble had now really arrived, insulated by financial security and floating on a creative high. Simon had been judged a winner by a jury of his peers and the future looked as bright and secure as it could for any twenty-seven-year-old on the planet. But Paul Simon had only another twelve months to go before the bubble burst.

The Boxer and the Bridge

As 1968 licked its wounds and limped into 1969, Simon completed a song that he was particularly proud of: 'The Boxer' marked the pinnacle of the Simon and Garfunkel sound and remains their finest song together. It was recorded, according to Simon, 'all over the place' – basic tracks in Nashville, the strings in New York, some vocals at a New York church; but despite its fragmentary gestation it still stands as the most cohesive and durable work of their partnership.

On its release in early 1969, there was much speculation that the song was nothing more than a veiled attack on Bob Dylan – his contemporaries in the Village compared the young Dylan to a boxer – and that the chorus (*lie la lie*) referred to Dylan's concealment of his real Robert Zimmerman persona. But to hail Simon's master-work as a sustained assault on his old nemesis was to belittle it. In later years, Simon admitted that the song was about himself and the criticisms that Simon and Garfunkel were attracting during that phase of their career. He told *Playboy*: 'I think I was reading the Bible around that time. That's where I think phrases such as "workman's wages" came from, and "seeking out the poorer quarters". That was biblical. I think the song was about *me*: everybody's beating me up, and I'm telling you now I'm going to go away if you don't stop!'

From the delicate guitar introduction to the dramatic orchestral climax five minutes later, 'The Boxer' remains one of the few classic rock songs from an era not exactly short of contenders. Simon, Garfunkel and Halee had managed to evoke the Wall of Sound that Phil Spector had patented, but they married it to a narrative worthy of the young Hemingway. 'The Boxer' is a song of optimism, but optimism only earned by riding the punches of a cold and uncaring world. The 'poor boy' of the song quit home at an early age to go on the road (like Simon's 'Duncan' three years later), but can only find solace in the company of strangers and whores on Seventh Avenue. Through a life buffeted and harried (listen to Simon's reading of the words '*cut him*'), the poor boy arrives at a clearing, with only his scars and punch-drunk memories to sustain him. It is a mixture of frustration, humility and dignity that causes him to cry out: '*I am leaving, I am leaving/But the fighter still remains!*' He recognizes that the essential something which makes him special, the spark of dignity, is still intact despite the onslaught of blows; he stands bloodied but unbowed. His cry of pain and realization offers a note of positivism: that however scuffed and beaten down the boxer gets, there is still a vestige of hope, of decency, left, and *that* is what will force him on to fly in the face of the society which has ignored him and constantly put him down.

In stereo, the song reveals innumerable riches; the peerless Simon and Garfunkel harmonies are diamond sharp, while Simon's acoustic guitar drives the song along in the time-honoured folk narrative tradition, but is emphasized by the thumping saxophone which underpins the song and the lush string arrangement which sustains the momentum of the long chorus. It was to be Simon and Garfunkel's only record of 1969. It was enough.

Paul had met and fallen in love with a southern belle called Peggy Harper; she was married at the time (a scenario Simon deals with in his song 'Train In The Distance' from 1983's *Hearts and Bones*). After her divorce the two were married and Simon found himself with a new partner and on the threshold of a new phase of his life.

Art Garfunkel had enjoyed the experience of working with Mike Nichols on *The Graduate* more than Simon, and was gratified to be invited to appear in his next film, which was to be a lavish adaptation of Joseph Heller's classic anti-war novel, *Catch-22*. Garfunkel was to play Nately, the eternal innocent of the novel. Simon was also supposed to appear in the film as Dunbar, but condensing Heller's 300-or-so-page novel into manageable screen time saw a number of minor characters being dropped, including Dunbar. Keen to consolidate the success of 'The Boxer', a new Simon and Garfunkel album was an obvious priority in 1969 and it was hoped that Garfunkel's role would only occupy him for three months. But with a multi-million dollar budget and extensive location work in Mexico and Italy, the film soon ran over. Nichols was under pressure, but the success of *The Graduate* was such that he was given *carte blanche*: for the first time since *Citizen Kane* in 1941, a studio relinquished the power of final cut to the director without having seen a finished foot of film. Ironically one of the stars of the film was Orson Welles, who had originally bought the film rights to the Heller novel, but sadly, as was so often the way with Welles' projects, he had been unable to raise the backing for his version and saw his option lapse.

One project which did occupy both Simon and Garfunkel during 1969 was their first TV special. Originally Simon and Garfunkel were to be guests on *The Bell Telephone Hour*, singing their greatest hits. The input from the two men soon proved that there was easily enough material for an hour-long special, which was to be funded to the tune of $600,000 by American Telephone & Telegraph (AT&T). Simon and Garfunkel saw their sixty minutes as a golden opportunity to reflect on the state of the nation as the decade drew to a turbulent end. Their songs would act as a vehicle for a deeper, more reflective look at a country at war with itself, coping with the Nixon/Agnew Presidency and still blindly forging ahead with the war in Vietnam.

The show was intended as a strongly critical, vehement political vehicle. While there was concert footage of Simon and Garfunkel – including the première of a new song, 'Bridge Over Troubled Water' – the heart of the show was a reflection on the divisive nature of American society. Images of popular heroes such as the Lone Ranger, *American Bandstand*'s Dick Clark and baseball player Mickey Mantle were juxtaposed with those of Lenny Bruce and Eugene McCarthy. There was newsreel footage of the Poor People's March on Washington, Martin Luther King, Robert Kennedy, Cesar Chavez and his striking farm workers and the psychedelic Nuremberg of Woodstock, all clashing with the bloody and vivid images of Vietnam. It was a resounding piece, a heartfelt impression of America, and one which proved too unsettling for AT&T. Stunned executives viewed the Special only days before its planned screening, happily anticipating an entertainment package along the lines of the *Andy Williams Show*. 'This is not what we contracted for,' commented AT&T aghast, 'we bought an entertainment show and they delivered their own personal, social and political views!' There was then a flurry of ultimatums, law suits and recriminations before the show, *Songs Of America*, was screened in emasculated form on 30th November, 1969, and was promptly binned.

Simon was outraged by the company's attitudes. In 1970 he was still smarting and told *Rolling Stone*: 'We decided to do a show on America, instead of just having a show with duets with Glen and the dance number . . . they said, "Your political philosophy is liberal humanism", so we said, "You mean to say that there are people who will object if we say you must feed everyone in this country?" . . . They just couldn't bear to look at King, couldn't bear to look at the Kennedys, couldn't bear to look at Chavez . . . they said they could live with the Lone Ranger. If we wanted to keep that in, it's all right!' So the one-time Lone Teen-Ranger grudgingly gratified the sponsors with the Lone Ranger, and the complacency of American TV audiences was left undisturbed.

Work on the follow-up to *Bookends*, though repeatedly delayed, eventually began in California where, midway through 1969 – while Art Garfunkel was still filming interiors for *Catch-22* – Paul and Peggy Simon hired a house. The house on Blue Jay Way in Los Angeles was coincidentally the same one in which George Harrison had written his contribution to 1967's *Magical Mystery Tour*. 'The Boxer' had been a full Simon-Garfunkel-Halee collaboration and Roy Halee was again around, as was Paul's brother Eddie, as basic song ideas and backing tracks were demoed for the new album; but with *Catch-22* eating up so much of Garfunkel's time, Simon was working largely alone on what proved to be Simon and Garfunkel's final album.

In October, with the filming of *Catch-22* finally finished and *Songs Of America* still to be screened, Simon and Garfunkel hit the road, for the first time complete with a touring band. Until then a Simon and Garfunkel concert had been just that, the two men occupying centre stage for ninety minutes, accompanied only by Simon's guitar. The autumn 1969 tour was with the same band who played on *Bridge Over Troubled Water*, and in Iowa they recorded a version of the Everly Brothers' 'Bye Bye Love' which wound up on the finished album – plans for a live album of the tour were announced at one point, but later withdrawn. 1969 ended, and still, nearly two years after *Bookends*, there was no sign of a new album. But early in 1970, Simon put in an uncharacteristic two-week burst of activity, during which he polished off 'Keep The Customer Satisfied' and 'Song For The Asking'; and by February *Bridge Over Troubled Water* was ready for release. To top the commercial success of *The Graduate* and the aesthetic merits of *Bookends* was a tall order, but Simon and Garfunkel managed to do both with an album and song which have become unquestionably their best-known works.

Quoted in presidential campaigns, heard at weddings and funerals, in lifts and shopping malls, recorded by over 200 different artists (including Simon's first hero Elvis Presley); 'Bridge Over

Troubled Water' saw Simon and Garfunkel become household names the world over. Ironically, *Bridge* proved to be their last studio album together, albeit one which ensured their joint career had a memorable climax.

The worldwide success of *Bridge Over Troubled Water* was due in part to the fact that it sold in its millions to people who don't normally buy records. Nearly twenty years on it has sold over eleven million copies. It won five Grammys (more than any other record had done before), and it was the first single and album to be simultaneously top of the American and British single and album charts. The song seemed like a clarion call for reason and calm, a beacon in the darkness, which ensured CBS 63699 was a permanent fixture on many record decks for much of the 1970s. By the end of its first year of release, Simon was estimated to have earned $7 million from the single alone. The album was a US Number 1 for ten weeks, while in the UK it held the top slot for an incredible seven months and remained in the charts for nearly six years. *Bridge Over Troubled Water* held sway over the world's charts for much of the decade, its success only eclipsed by *Saturday Night Fever, Rumours,* and *Tapestry,* by Paul Simon's former partner Carole King. Later on, of course, these were all left standing by the success of Michael Jackson's *Thriller,* which shattered all previous records and sold a staggering thirty-eight million worldwide.

The roots of 'Bridge Over Troubled Water' were in Gospel, a tradition which had always fascinated Simon. It is to his credit that Simon recognized the impertinence of two rich white boys from Queens singing the music born from the unimaginable suffering of an entire people. Simon tailored the song to suit himself and Garfunkel. Although some may call it watered-down Gospel, he was frightened of seeming presumptuous and followed his own conscience. Simon cites as his direct inspiration a Gospel song called 'Oh Mary Don't You Weep' by the Swan Silvertones and their distinctive singer the Reverend Claude Juter: 'Had it not been for him, I would never have written "Bridge Over Troubled Water". . . . The guy has probably the best falsetto voice in the world, and somewhere in the middle he scat sings "I'll be your bridge over deep water if you trust in my name". ' Simon later repaid his debt to the Rev. Juter when he asked him to sing on 'Take Me To The Mardi Gras' on Simon's second solo album in 1973.

Of all the songs to date, Simon was proudest of his melody for 'Bridge'. In its initial stages the song was simply known as 'Hymn', and there was some confusion about the title when assigning the song to be transcribed for strings: the arranger, Jimmy Haskell, misheard the title and scored it as 'Like A Pitcher Of Water'. Simon had the original string arrangement with that title framed! The song originally had only two verses, but Simon added the third verse at short notice in the studio. At the time many people interpreted the line '*sail on silvergirl*' as referring to a hypodermic syringe; in fact it was a reference to his wife panicking at finding two or three grey hairs one morning, but as late as 1982 a trio of pastors were still citing the line as an example of Simon and Garfunkel condoning the use of drugs!

The arrangement owes much to a Phil Spector production of 'Ol' Man River' for the Righteous Brothers. In true Spector style he saved up his final punch as a knockout blow, giving the 'brothers' only very sparse backing, until the final chorus unleashed his customary Wall of Sound to sing '*ol' man river*' to the fade; and it was this idea of restraint and contrasting impact which appealed to Simon and Garfunkel. It is hard to imagine anyone else but Art Garfunkel tackling the epic vocals of 'Bridge Over Troubled Water', but at the time he was unsure whether he could handle the onerous task; however, Simon insisted that it was the purity of Art's singing which would give the song its full impact.

A number of people noticed the similarities between 'Bridge' and the Beatles valedictory 'Let It Be' when it was released the following month. Simon told *Rolling Stone*: 'They are very similar songs . . . sort of in their general musical feel, and lyrically. They're both sort of hopeful songs, and resting, peaceful songs . . . it's one of those weird things, and it happened simultaneously.' The uplifting spirituality of these two songs paved the way for many other quasi–religious efforts. The peace and love elements of the late 60s had served only to highlight the spiritual vacuum which they had been attempting to fill. By the early 70s this search for a reason to believe was evinced by popular songs such as 'Amazing Grace', 'My Sweet Lord', 'Morning Has Broken' and the ubiquitous 'Desiderata'.

The epic title track and 'The Boxer' dominate the *Bridge Over Troubled Water* album; two stirring and immensely moving songs imbued with a majesty and force which few in popular music could match. The only other track on the album that comes close to the power of these two is the wistful 'Only Living Boy In New York', a Simon solo effort, written about Garfunkel while the latter was marooned down in Mexico filming *Catch-22*. Perhaps Simon already knew the writing was on the wall for their partnership: he recalls the Tom and Jerry pseudonyms – Artie was Tom Graph – and the song stands as a touching farewell to the partner who had been at his side throughout their inexorable rise.

Simon had been cajoled by Garfunkel into writing a song about the architect Frank Lloyd Wright for the final track on side one, but ironically it is in effect another song about the parting of the ways. At the conclusion of 'So Long Frank Lloyd Wright', buried way down in the mix, as the multi-tracked Simon and Garfunkel vocals resonate, Garfunkel reflectively and sadly sings *'So long, so long . . .'* while Simon can be heard to call out *'So long already Artie!'*

'Keep The Customer Satisfied' is a brassy, hard-rocking number, the all-too-rare sound of Simon and Garfunkel letting their hair down; but even in this apparently throw-away song, enormous care has been taken over the lyrics, which feature a typically audacious Simon rhyme: *'I get slandered, libelled/I hear words I never heard in the Bible'*. 'Baby Driver' is another rocking effort which is superficially autobiographical – though whether Simon's mother was in the naval reserve remains unconfirmed to this day! Simon called 'Cecilia' 'a little piece of magical fluff'; the song came about by Simon playing around with percussion over a basic backing track and singing the first lines that came into his head.

Still drawing on his European experiences of five years before, Simon took an original eighteenth-century Peruvian folk song called 'El Condor Pasa' which he had heard Los Incas playing in Paris. He kept the original title and invited Los Incas to play on the backing track, but replaced the original story of Tupac Amaru's revolt against the Spanish with some trite lyrics of his own. Already Simon's interest in non-rock musical forms was manifest and 'Why Don't You Write Me' was a first unhappy stab at reggae, which he would tackle far more convincingly two years later on 'Mother and Child Reunion'. The album's final song is the suitably valedictory 'A Song For The Asking', significantly a Simon solo effort which finds him keen to change his ways.

The growing estrangement between Simon and Garfunkel, which had started primarily as a result of Art's seemingly endless involvement with *Catch-22* and his consequent signing for Nichols' fourth film *Carnal Knowledge*, had finally come to a head while they were putting together *Bridge Over Troubled Water*. Simon insisted that the album should feature twelve tracks and that the last should be a vitriolic song called 'Cuba Si, Nixon No', which attacked the President's ruling that no American citizen could visit Castro's Cuba. Garfunkel disliked the song and refused to sing it; he was set instead on substituting a Bach chorale which Simon felt was wholly unsuitable for a Simon and Garfunkel album. They reached a total impasse – symbolic of their crumbling relationship and their increasing inability to communicate with each other. The compromise was not a happy one, Simon told Jon Landau in 1972: 'We were fighting over which was gonna be the twelfth song, and then I said, "Fuck it, put it out with eleven songs, if that's the way it is!" We were at the end of our energies over that.'

Simon and Garfunkel toured to promote the *Bridge* album. They played to an ecstatic crowd at London's Royal Albert Hall in April 1970; the touring band was left behind, and again it was just the two of them, with pianist Larry Knechtel coming on to accompany Art on 'Bridge'. But it couldn't last – more than fifteen years after first singing together, they played their last concert in the summer of 1970 on their home ground of Forest Hills; they concluded with the Penguins' 'Earth Angel' and donated $10,000 of the proceeds to Cesar Chavez.

If the partnership had endured, Garfunkel was keen to move closer toward his own innately conservative and lush style of music, but they could no longer compromise and it was perhaps a relief for Garfunkel that he was now free to pursue his acting career. CBS, however, were understandably upset at the prospect of Simon and Garfunkel never recording together again, and Simon found himself in the invidious position of having to top *Bridge Over Troubled Water* alone.

The partnership had begun as Tom and Jerry in the rock and roll mayhem of 1957 with the Everly Brothers as their inspiration, and ended fifteen years later with Simon and Garfunkel's names soldered together as inseparably as Lennon and McCartney's. In the interim they had become millionaires several times over. From street corner hops to concert halls around the world, the strain had taken its toll on the friendship. Both saw the split as inevitable and publicly it was conducted with dignity, but in private the bitterness had been brewing and it was a rancorous relationship which simmered even longer than their partnership had lasted.

The Simon and Garfunkel split ironically presaged that of their role models, the Everly Brothers, whom Simon acknowledged as inspirational. 'Without the Everly Brothers there would have been no Simon and Garfunkel.' The brothers' sibling rivalry would come to a head on stage three years later in June 1973, when Phil stormed off in mid-song and didn't speak to his brother again for a decade. The Everlys did, however, get back together for a triumphant reunion in 1983 and have been working happily together ever since; it was a source of great delight to Simon that they sang back-up vocals on the title track of his *Graceland* album. Simon and Garfunkel, though, never did regain that closeness – as with Lennon and McCartney who split at much the same time and were sniping constantly at each other throughout the 70s, the ties that bound had become a noose.

Looking back on the Simon and Garfunkel years, Simon realized that increasingly he had had to reconcile his instincts about his own songs with Garfunkel, who wanted to take the music in a direction which Simon didn't necessarily agree with. It was in collaboration with Roy Halee and each other that Simon and Garfunkel developed their musical identity; with Simon's strongly constructed songs as a basis, they would all pitch in with ideas for arrangement and developments. CBS producer Bob Johnston – who numbered Bob Dylan, Leonard Cohen and Johnny Cash amongst his charges – also worked with Simon and Garfunkel between 1965 and 1967, but Simon has since been scathing about his role. He told Lon Goddard: 'Johnston? As a producer? He was only there to find out who wanted a chicken salad sandwich!'

The internal dynamics of the three-way collaboration remain impossible to disentangle, with Simon's perception of events shifting as the years go by. In the early 70s he did admit to some creative input from Garfunkel and Halee: 'Each person had a relatively equal say, so in other words, if Roy and Artie said, "Let's do a long ending on 'The Boxer' " I said, "Two out of three" and did it their way. I didn't say "Hey this is my song I don't want to do it like that". ' By 1984 Simon was telling *Playboy*: 'I lied. He lied. We said, "We're Simon and Garfunkel; I write the songs, Artie arranges them". We would parade that. It was a joint statement all through the sixties. Everyone believed it, and of course it was never true. . . . I wanted to get away from the big orchestrations . . . make simpler, funkier records.'

The resentment was not just a consequence of the long and tortuous sessions which went into a Simon and Garfunkel album; Simon reflected in a Jon Landau interview: 'Many times on stage when I'd be sitting at the side and Larry Knechtel would be playing the piano and Artie would be singing "Bridge", people would stamp and cheer when it was over. And I would think, "That's my song, man, thank you very much, I wrote that song"!' Simon the composer felt an understandable sense of bitterness, but then Artie the singer also made the song what it was; it is tempting to think that perhaps deep down Simon knew and resented that fact. For years many people though that the two wrote their songs together, probably because Garfunkel *looked* like a writer. During his long, confessional interview with *Playboy* in 1984, Simon himself admitted: 'He was angelic looking, with fluffy blonde hair. And he was tall and thin and he had this voice, and it seemed right. He *should* have been the one who wrote the songs. That body *should* have contained that talent. And I think that's part of what caused him anguish too.'

Simon had little interest in touring; he felt that it was in the intensity of the studio that his songs were forged and that the partnership really came alive. He was always dismissive of Simon and Garfunkel as a live attraction, and of the alleged benefits of the road: 'Simon and Garfunkel had a peculiar type of groupies. We had the poetic groupies. The girls that followed us around weren't necessarily looking to sleep with us as much as they were looking to read their poetry or discuss literature . . . I wasn't into picking up girls on the road. Couldn't do it. Too embarrassing for me. I wasn't interested in their poetry either!' The aimless monotony of life on the road did however provide artistic inspiration, and Simon would brilliantly tackle it ten years later in his film *One Trick Pony*.

There were some perks of the rock and roll lifestyle which Simon didn't ignore, however, and for escape there were always drugs, particularly at the height of the Summer of Love, when all sorts of narcotic Nirvanas and acid Arcadias were on offer. Simon experimented with LSD and was not averse to marijuana, but did not find that either particularly stimulated him as a writer; by the end of the Simon and Garfunkel partnership he had eschewed drugs and given up smoking, only to immerse himself in analysis.

There was a very particular type of pressure that haunted talented individuals like Paul Simon. Judith Piepe, who had kept in close touch with him since 1965 when he used her flat as a base in London, reflected on him as a person: 'Like all singer–songwriters, difficult. A performer, a singer, *has* to be extrovert. . . . But a writer is introvert, because you can't create in a crowd. And a singer–songwriter is always on a horrible see-saw. It makes people difficult, irritable and a little hard to live with. . . . Paul was as moody as any songwriter, because it's a sort of split personality. . . . A boy who is 5'1″ and is a New York Jew *has* to be ambitious. . . . English people go to the dentist. Americans have analysis. English women talk to their hairdressers, English men talk to their barman and New York Americans talk to their analyst!' Simon found solace in analysis; he used the dialogue as an opportunity to analyse and examine the dichotomy of his immense wealth and success with his personal dissatisfaction and corrosive unhappiness. The experience was particularly valuable in conquering a case of writer's block immediately after *One Trick Pony*.

By 1970, Paul Simon's ambition had carried him from a comfortable, middle-class background in New York to a pop career at age sixteen; to university and to a living in the folk clubs of Europe; to the experience of having a Number 1 hit single and being able to consolidate his reputation with a series of beautifully crafted, brilliantly produced albums. He had accrued a cupboardful of Grammies and a wall dripping with gold discs. But in the immediate aftermath of the Simon and Garfunkel split, Paul Simon still needed more.

Rhymin' Simon

The air of optimism which usually heralds a new decade was sadly absent from 1970. The idealism and optimism which had seemed so buoyant during the late 60s was evaporating. With Nixon installed in the White House and laying the foundations for his second term, rebellion was no longer an easily marketable commodity; a new conservatism was fast becoming entrenched. The vanquished positivism was nowhere more felt than in the first year of the new decade when the Beatles split. The group had come to represent the apotheosis of pop culture, and the inherent energy and possibility of change symbolized by the Beatles had borne us through the 60s; but now they went their separate ways in a bitter, protracted dispute which saw the idealism of Apple replaced with a vulgar and atavistic grab for bucks. To purge himself of the Beatle experience, John Lennon released in 1970 the cathartic *Plastic Ono Band*, a pioneering work of the singer–songwriter era.

To protest at the escalation of the Vietnam war under Nixon, which by then was spilling into Cambodia and laying the foundations for the fanatical genocide of Pol Pot, students took over their campuses, and at Kent State four protesting teenagers were murdered by the National Guard. The establishment, banished to the wings for so long, was back centre-stage and cracking down with an iron fist. Their spokesmen being systematically picked off, American youth was in danger of becoming disenfranchised again: Dylan had gone into a three-year retreat after a series of patchy albums, drugs which had seemed to offer so much now took away Hendrix and Janis Joplin, and isolationist stadium rock was ushered in by bands like Emerson, Lake and Palmer, Crosby, Stills, Nash and Young, and Led Zeppelin. The Rolling Stones, rowdy street-fighting men, were quietly slipping into tax exile. The split of Simon and Garfunkel was not to be measured in such apocalyptic terms, but with the announcement that they would no longer be working together, a sense of security was lost.

Musically the early 70s were characterized by a sense of reluctant acquiesence rather than energetic rebellion. The enervating world party of the 60s was over and there was just enough energy left for tears before bedtime. The 'Me' Generation was coming of age; Simon's old Queens colleague Carole King unleashed the gentle giant *Tapestry*, while Joni Mitchell's introspective ballads fed a hungry new audience, eager to avoid overt politicization and following the urge to look inwards. That popular movement of the singer-songwriter found its perfect symbol in James Taylor, whose *Sweet Baby James* album of 1970 established him as a pensive, withdrawn and tortured artist. Madness and revenge were in the air, George Jackson was cut down in a prison rebellion in 1971, Angela Davis was chased across the country, William Calley was convicted of the massacre of Vietnamese civilians. It was no wonder that people turned away from the world and started looking inside themselves for the answers. Simon's line from 'The Only Living Boy In New York' seemed curiously apposite: '*Half of the time we're gone, and we don't know where!*'

After the pressures of Simon and Garfunkel, and with the un-avoidable prospect of a solo career, Simon gingerly tested the water with a brief appearance at Shea Stadium in August 1970 as part of a concert to mark the twenty-fifth anniversary of the atomic bombing of Hiroshima. The show was not a success. Simon played to a restless crowd, whose attitude was aggravated by heavy-handed policing; Simon played a couple of familiar Simon and Garfunkel numbers, but stormed off during 'Scarborough Fair'. Apart from that, he was taking a well-deserved rest from performing. He was happily married to Peggy, who encouraged him in his writing and helped him consolidate his belief in himself and his abilities.

As a safety valve from writing and prior to putting himself under the microscope with his solo relaunch, Simon undertook some lectures for songwriting workshops at New York University during the summer of 1971. Among the students he taught were the Roche Sisters, Maggie and Terre, and singer-songwriter Melissa Manchester, who remembers that as a teacher, Simon was nervous. He listened to the students' songs and offered suggestions and criticism, often dissecting the lyrics and drawing comparisons with his own work, while offering autobiographical insights into how his own work progressed and from where he drew his inspiration. 'He told us about the first time he ever met Bob Dylan,' recalled Manchester. 'He said he went over to his house all excited and the place was a total mess, with junk all over and wrinkled old scraps of paper covering the floor. Dylan kept walking around the room talking and thinking out loud. Paul followed, picking up every loose scrap of paper he could find – anything with words on it – and stuffed them in his pockets. He said he was dying to find out how Dylan did it!'

The contrast between the two pre-eminent American lyricists of the 60s could not be more stark: Dylan rarely revised any work, and his studio technique was simply to get it right as quickly as possible or forget it! Compare that with Simon and his punctilious attention to works in progress, endlessly revising and rewriting, spending months in the studio to try and attain perfection in his work, but perversely never seeming satisfied with the end results. The difference in technique of the two artists may, incidentally, explain the wealth of Dylan bootleg material available compared to the paucity of Simon's. But comparisons between the two are rarely fruitful. Dylan certainly inspired Simon at the beginning, but by the time of *Parsley, Sage, Rosemary and Thyme* Simon was moving away and creating his own polished style. The best of Paul Simon's work with Simon and Garfunkel is characterized by a meticulousness which Dylan could never approach; his writing style was a shotgun spraying pellets everywhere, while Simon's – to stretch the analogy – was a hand-crafted Purdey. It was only later during his cathartic *Playboy* interview of 1984 that Simon spoke finally about his feelings towards Dylan, admiring the 'moving lyrics' of 'Boots Of Spanish Leather', 'Girl From The North Country' and 'Don't Think Twice It's Alright': 'It's funny to hear myself saying that. It may be the first generous thing I've ever said about Bob Dylan. In the early days, I was always too angry about being compared with him. And then, he's hard to be generous to, because he's so ungenerous himself.'

While the public bickering between Simon and Dylan continued unabated, Dylan paid his occasional protégé a double-edged compliment by recording a bizarre version of 'The Boxer' for his pick and mix *Self Portrait* in 1970. Double-tracking himself (the Dylan Brothers?), Dylan showed a complete lack of sensitivity in his reading of Simon's finest song of the period: Emmylou Harris actually interpreted the song far more sensitively a decade later on *Roses In The Snow*.

Latterly, Simon has been impressed by songwriters like Elvis Costello, Lou Reed, David Byrne and Bruce Springsteen: 'He's made those South Jersey highways, the cars, into an archetypal, almost mythic form of expression.' Simon also professed admiration for John Lennon's best work, vignettes like 'In My Life' and

'Strawberry Fields Forever' – slices of autobiography distanced by drugs or memory. Like Lennon, who was unable to make up his mind about whether to be included in or out of the 'Revolution', Simon recently decided – on *The Concert In Central Park* – that life looked 'better' in black and white, whereas the original 'Kodachrome' lyrics in 1973 had *'everything looks worse in black and white'*.

Like Lennon, hopes and aspirations are an integral part of Simon's life and work; on 'A Hazy Shade Of Winter' he sings *'hang on to your hopes my friend'* while Jonah Levin in *One Trick Pony* sings: *'No one lets their dreams be taken lightly'*. As he edges towards fifty, however, Paul Simon feels the pain of the world less acutely and recognizes that as an individual, personal blessings must be counted: *'I don't know a dream that's not been shattered, or driven to its knees/But it's all right, it's all right/We've lived so well so long'*, ('American Tune', 1973). With the birth of their sons, both proud fathers were moved to write two of their most beautiful songs: Lennon's 'Beautiful Boy' and Simon's 'Saint Judy's Comet' signalled that their angry idealism had grown into tender hope. The dreams, though, will never die, as Simon sings on 'Train In The Distance' (1983): *'the thought that life could be better is woven indelibly into our hearts and our brains'*.

Another unavoidable Beatles comparison is the recent career of Paul McCartney with that of Paul Simon: by the age of thirty, both men could comfortably have retired for life, having already assured themselves of a lasting place in rock iconography. They were unable, however, to rely on former glories and both needed to prove to themselves that they could go it alone. Simon and McCartney are undeniably masters of the popular song, continuing to offer work which they firmly believe ranks alongside their very best of the 60s. Songwriting is, after all, their job, their career, and they will do their best to ensure that every release contains the hallmarks of quality the audience has come to expect. At least the audience no longer requires them to be role models or leaders and can simply enjoy their ability to articulate universal feelings in an easily accessible form.

In other genres, Simon's artistic heroes include novelists John Cheever and Saul Bellow and the film-maker Woody Allen. Indeed both Simon and his second wife, Carrie Fisher, have appeared in Allen films, and the similarities between the two men's work is marked. Both men's best work concerns their own milieu, though their observations seem remote due to a painful sense of self-awareness which they share. Both are east coast intellectuals who reluctantly travel to the west coast to work. While the teenage Paul Simon was hustling record producers in the Brill Building, Allen, six years his senior, was doorstepping TV producers with his gags and scripts. Allen's 1979 film *Manhattan* is the cinematic equivalent of Simon's *Still Crazy After All These Years* album of 1975; they are confident, assured works from Upper West Side New York neurotics dealing with the foibles of coteries of their contemporaries.

The isolationism they have in common sees Allen and Simon trapped in creative bubbles with a rather shaky belief in themselves; Allen has almost single-handedly kept New York psychiatrists in business, while Simon has also undergone sporadic bouts of analysis. One of the recurring themes in Paul Simon's work is the tight rein which needs to be kept on cool rationality, and the delicate balance between social sanity and private madness. Many people, like the character in 'Stranded In A Limousine' (1977) recognize themselves as 'naturally crazy'. That tightrope is something that Simon focuses on again in 'Everything Put Together Falls Apart' (1972): *'some folks are crazy, others walk that borderline'.* Similar concerns are evident on songs such as 'Paranoia Blues' (1972) and 'Still Crazy After All These Years' (1975); while the two versions of 'Think Too Much' (1983) are the closest glimpse we get of Simon's view of his own psyche and his inability to act spontaneously: *'maybe I think too much for my own good'* – though at the end of the day Paul Simon can recognize a hawk from a handsaw better than most!

In 1980, the character of Jonah Levin in *One Trick Pony* was singing: *'Once I was crazy and my ace in the hole/Was that I knew that I was crazy/So I never lost my self-control'.* Losing that self-control is the one thing that seems to fill Simon with dread. The desire for control sometimes borders on obsession, ensuring that in his songs – as he would wish for in life – nothing put together ever falls apart. But as everyone knows, real life isn't that easy to control, and sadly both his attempts at marriage have ended in divorce.

In popular song mythology love and marriage 'go together like a horse and carriage', but in Simon's songs they seem to have little in common. While his love songs have been deservedly acclaimed, his treatment of marriage on vinyl seems to concentrate on the dry legal aspects of that institution – perhaps a vestige of his six-month-long legal training. In 'America' the couple decide to *'marry their fortunes together','we were married on a rainy day . . . we signed the papers and we drove away'* ('I Do It For Your Love', 1975), and on 'Train In The Distance' he talks of *'disagreements about the meaning of a marriage contract'*. Sad reminders that despite his wealth of talent – and just plain wealth! – Simon has found that lasting happiness within marriage has eluded him. 'Congratulations' in 1972 is also a poignant reflection on failed marriages and finds Simon wistfully asking, *'can a man and a woman live together in peace?'*

As with many writers, much of Simon's early work is autobio-graphical: 'He Was My Brother' was an incensed reaction to the mindless murder of a friend by racist bigots, 'A Church Is Burning' condemns arsonists in the Deep South. What Simon calls his 'English songs' – 'Kathy's Song', 'Homeward Bound', 'A Most Peculiar Man', 'April Come She Will' and others – were forged while he was perfecting his craft, and the first two were inspired directly by his love for and the distance from Kathy. He has chron-icled his marriages and the birth in 1972 of his son Harper by his first wife, Peggy, although his early life with his parents has only been shadowily alluded to in 'Baby Driver', 'Late In The Evening' (1980) and 'Loves Me Like A Rock' (1975). His life in the music business and his experience of the fickleness of fame were dealt with on the film and album of *One Trick Pony* in 1980, though Simon never fell victim to the whinging self-pity of stardom typified by early 1970s' singer-songwriters like James Taylor ('Hey Mister That's Me Up On The Jukebox') and Joni Mitchell ('Free Man In Paris').

Despite the number of works rooted in first-hand experience, Simon as songwriter was always on the outside looking in, rather than on the inside looking out. The angst-ridden diary of Dylan circa *Blood On The Tracks* and Elvis Costello on *Armed Forces* was not for him. Even Simon's most overtly autobiographical collec-tions have a sense of distance which ensures that the songs will stand on their own merits. To produce these beautifully crafted, finely tuned works however, Simon has sacrificed a degree of emotional involvement which can lead to his work being viewed as clinical. While there is much to admire in the craftsmanship, there is little to involve the listener. At their cathartic best Lennon, Dylan, Costello and Tom Waits leave blood on their tracks; with Paul Simon there's always the impression of a bandage close at hand! That is not necessarily to denigrate his work however, for while he may emphatically refute that 'My Little Town' (1975), for example, is directly autobiographical, there is no denying the acuteness of his vision, or his ability to convey the environment and circumstances of the song's character. Simon puts himself at a safe distance from his song's protagonists, but the distancing lends a sense of perspective which enhances rather than diminishes; as a 'poet of alienation', it would perhaps be wrong for Simon to get close to his characters. But as R. D. Laing wrote: 'We are born into a world where alienation awaits us.'

It is that very discipline and objectivity, coupled with Simon's innate song-writing mastery, which will see his finest work last long after the foibles and fads of pop music have been forgotten; his best work will be as much a part of the fabric of American popular music as Gershwin.

By the time of his first major work, 'The Sound Of Silence', Simon's songs were already evincing a hallmark: the ability to distance himself, a commentator rather than a character. The song's first verse echoes the songwriter's craft, 'a vision planted' in his brain, left gestating, later to be revised and painstakingly honed, the punctiliousness even carrying through to the actual process of recording and lasting until the song was fully realized.

On eloquent, narrative works such as 'Save The Life of My Child', 'The Boxer', 'The Only Living Boy In New York' and 'Duncan' (1972), Simon had found his own voice, articulate, poised and confident, with an ear for dialogue, an understanding of his characters and the discipline to develop the narrative clearly and cogently. It is a tradition of the folk song which Simon utilized to his own ends in the pop mainstream.

By the time of *Bookends* Simon's work was displaying the strict attention to detail and discipline one expects from printed verse. The suite on that album's first side shows his keenness to experiment with verse forms, rhyme and metre, from the interior monologue of 'Overs' to the open letter of 'America'. Simon was one of the few rock 'poets' successfully to integrate blank verse into a format which has always relied heavily on rhyme, with 'America' as the finest example.

Simon had studied literature at university – Robert Frost and Emily Dickinson are name checked on 'The Dangling Conversation' – and like labelmate Leonard Cohen, Simon brought distinctly poetic elements to the rock song. Simon, however, considered the music equally important and was thus able to add an extra dimension to his lyrics, while Cohen tended to settle for drearily accompanied readings.

All manner of literary devices enhance and embellish Simon's songs; fond of alliteration, he uses it to great effect in lines such as *'dappled and drowsy'*, *'flashing . . . fireflies'*, *'the look of lovelight'* and *'cabinet cold'*. The rhyming, too, is frequently imaginative: Bible/libel, Bible/survival, Lord/reward, lost/Pentecost and astute/institute. Improbable words like 'paraphernalia', 'litigation', 'misconstrued' and 'bodegas' also find sanctuary in the songs of Paul Simon; and he is an acute judge of the *mot juste* as in 'A *Hazy* Shade Of Winter', the *'stony sky'* and the *'naked light'*. Simon also makes use of aural puns, *'a Nikon camera'* on 'Kodachrome' could well be 'an icon', *'crazy motion'* from 'Something So Right' (1975) sounds like 'emotion', while in 'Cecilia' *'I fall on the floor and I laughing'* comes across as 'die laughing'.

In Simon's early 'alienation' songs the spectre of T. S. Eliot hovers. 'The Sound Of Silence' echoes Eliot's 'The Love Song of J. Alfred Prufrock' and 'Rhapsody on a Windy Night'; 'The Dangling Conversation' finds Simon noting *'our place with bookmarkers, to measure what we've lost'*, while Eliot conveys that same sense of domestic claustrophobia with 'I have measured out my life with coffee spoons'. Even as late as 'Crazy Love Vol. II' from *Graceland* (1986) Simon writes of a character *'sad as a lonely wrinkled balloon'*, surely subconsciously echoing Eliot's 'old man with wrinkled female breasts' in 'The Waste Land'.

For someone so versed in and respectful of pop history, Simon's work owes remarkably little to its traditions. Little influence from country and western or blues can be detected – not for Simon the tormented drifting and plaintive blues of Hank Williams or Robert Johnson; rather the assured poise of a Cole.Porter or Lorenz Hart. But it is undeniably in the rock mainstream that Simon has worked, save for occasional 'classical' forays with Leonard Bernstein or Philip Glass, and his appreciation of pop history is manifest. Out-and-out pop clichés, when used by Simon, are usually tongue in cheek, as in 'We've Got a Groovey Thing Goin' ', 'Cecilia' and 'Baby Driver'; very consciously used to underline a point about the triteness of pop songs. Simon would be the first to defend the importance of, say, the Penguins' 'Earth Angel', the Everly Brothers' 'Bye Bye Love' or any one of a hundred other pop classics; but he sees it as his role to carry the tradition forward.

Simon's lyrics are frequently embellished by an invigorating use of melody and approach to song structures, and his interest in, and knowledge of, musical forms which fall outside the pop idiom are unique. From early on in his career, Simon was keen to explore and expand the possibilities of sound in the studio; and throughout his solo career he has successfully experimented with unfamiliar strands – culminating, of course, in his audacious use of the music of black South Africa on *Graceland*. Like an alchemist he distils the essence of other musical traditions and creates his own synthesis. Simon's cleverness lies in his managing to avoid a clumsy graft and create a seamless whole.

As a writer with so many songs now being a part of the public consciousness, it is remarkable that Simon is not more prolific. Slaving over the perfect union of lyric and melody, his output is tiny: together, Simon and Garfunkel recorded a mere five albums, and only had complete control over the last three. Even *Bookends*, their finest album, was filled out by the inclusion of four old singles. Simon, though, was never one to confuse quantity with quality; and his process of songwriting, of honing and slaving to obtain exactly the right arrangement and production, ensures that even his early songs seem as fresh today as they did over twenty years ago. While Simon himself may squirm at the naïvety of 'I Am A Rock' or 'The Dangling Conversation', and view the lush romanticism of 'For Emily . . .' with scepticism, there is no doubt that they still have charm, and their importance at the time – when rock music was attempting to find a voice and offer a direction – was inestimable.

After the break-up of Simon and Garfunkel, there was no obvious incentive for Simon ever to record again. 'Bridge Over Troubled Water' alone had assured him of a healthy income for the rest of his life, and Simon was never terribly motivated by profit. Critics of his songs with Garfunkel had called them anodyne folk protestors, accused them of bandwagon jumping, of questioning but never supplying answers and of being the acceptable face of youth rebellion; now unencumbered by a partner from whom he was growing increasingly distant, Simon had the opportunity to allow his writing to develop a harder, more cutting edge.

Paul Simon was convinced that his new songs would be as rewarding to him as Simon and Garfunkel's had been to the world; but not everyone shared his conviction, as he remembered to *Rolling Stone* in 1972: 'Clive [Davis] once said to me, "Simon and Garfunkel is a household word. No matter however successful you'll be, you'll never be as successful as Simon and Garfunkel!" So I said, "Yeah, like Dean Martin and Jerry Lewis. Don't tell me that. . . . How do you know what I'll do? I don't even know what I'm gonna do in the next decade of my life. It could be maybe my greatest time of work. Maybe I'm finished. Maybe I'm not gonna do my thing until I'm fifty. People will say then, funny thing was, in his youth, he sang with a group. He sang popular songs in the sixties!"'

American Tunes

In retrospect the decade's music was slow in getting rolling, although 1972 saw some important auguries: David Bowie released the seminal *Ziggy Stardust* album and John Hammond signed Bruce Springsteen to CBS. *Paul Simon* began with the then unfamiliar reggae rhythms of Kingston, Jamaica and a promise not to offer 'false hope'. By the album's conclusion, it was obvious that any hope invested in Simon would not be misplaced. Provisionally entitled *Duncan* (after the album's second song) Simon settled on the highly original title *Paul Simon* for his first solo album in seven years. It was released early in 1972, and was Number 1 on the US album charts within weeks of its release. Simon had been impressed with the funkiness of Ry Cooder's 1970 debut album, and he was determined to capture a harder edge on his solo work, impatient to move away from the lustrous sound which had epitomized Simon and Garfunkel. Garfunkel, on the other hand, retained and even developed the lushness, as his debut solo album of 1973, *Angel Clare*, testifies.

Recorded all over the world, in Jamaica, Paris, New York, Los Angeles and San Francisco, *Paul Simon* displayed the composer's virtuosity at working in virtually any musical style, and emphasized a looser, funkier feel; his new songs displayed a lyrical inventiveness which showed that two years on Simon had lost none of his acute perception. The album's opening track and first single, 'Mother and Child Reunion', was weirdly inspired by a chicken and egg dish Simon had enjoyed in a Chinese restaurant! From such humble gastronomic beginnings he crafted a beautiful and haunting contemplation on the intimations of mortality – some of the lyrics were actually based on a dog of the Simons' which had recently died. The lyrics deal poignantly with the loss of someone close to you: the finality of death is tempered by the realization that reconciliation lies *'only a motion away'*.

Travel had not only increased Simon's musical vocabulary but had also broadened his perspective on the world. It is worth remembering that Simon was the first major white rock and roll artist to utilize reggae rhythms – *Rolling Stone* was so uncertain of the genre that during their 1972 interview with him they consistently refer to it as 'reggal'! It took Bob Marley and the Wailers' classic *Catch A Fire* album of 1973 to bring reggae to the world, and white stars like Eric Clapton and Paul McCartney to popularize it, but Simon had been there first. Simon had fond memories of Desmond Dekker and Millie Small ska and bluebeat singles, which were popular when he was in England in the mid-60s. But by the beginning of the 70s in England, reggae had been hijacked rather ironically as 'skinhead music' – dance music for the working-class cult, which had emerged as a reaction against the middle-class hippies, but was later tainted by the racist overtones which soon became its main preoccupation. At the time it was frowned on by the intellectual rock critics; but after dipping his toe in the water with the shuffling reggae-inspired rhythm on 'Why Don't You Write Me', Simon was determined to get a more authentic reggae sound for 'Mother and Child Reunion'.

Simon had been impressed by Jimmy Cliff's single, 'Vietnam', and wanted to record his own song at the same studio and enlist the cream of Kingston's session players to perform on the track. The sessions were not without incident. The players assembled at Dynamic Studios were used to bashing through as many as six tracks a day, getting $10 per song, and happily quitting late in the evening with a cool $60. They had never come across anyone with Simon's pedantic approach to recording, and were concerned that he was taking the best part of a week to do just one track! Ruffled feathers were soon calmed, though, and the session continued. Interestingly, one of the backing singers on the song is Cissy Houston, mother of the now mega Whitney.

The funky edge Simon wished to percolate his music with was also apparent on the jumping 'Paranoia Blues' which has some inspired bottleneck playing from Stefan Grossman. 'Me and Julio Down By The Schoolyard' is a masterly pop song. Borrowing this time from infectious Latin rhythms, it gave 1972 one of its quirkiest hit singles. Similar to 'Cecilia', the song started life as a tape loop Simon was so happy with that he knocked off some lyrics to fit. He confessed that he had no idea what '*the mama saw*' that was against the law, except that it was probably something sexual. Simon's effervescent rhymes ensure that the song remains a constant delight.

Originally planned as the title track, 'Duncan' was another striking song, which again displayed Simon's penchant for utilizing non-rock instrumentation to gain an idiosyncratic sound. In the context of Simon and Garfunkel, one can imagine the song as a lavish orchestral piece held together by Simon's folk guitar style. Here the backing is supplied by Los Incas, with whom Simon had kept in touch since meeting them in Paris in 1965, and who had supplied the backing track for the limp 'El Condor Pasa' in 1970. Lincoln Duncan is the laconic hero of one of Simon's finest ever narrative songs; employing deft imagery and an economic sense of lyric, Simon vividly portrays the life of an underdog and climaxes with his first sexual triumph, leaving the listener with a precise feeling of time, place and character.

There was some dead wood on the debut: 'Run That Body Down' is a small idea stretched over three verses and an unmemorable melody. 'Hobo's Blues', however, is a worthwhile piece of jazz swing, in which Simon comfortably and literally plays second fiddle to the legendary violinist Stephane Grappelli who had scored such success with gypsy guitarist Django Reinhardt in Paris in the 1930s.

Perhaps the most significant achievement of the album from Simon's viewpoint was that it finally laid to rest the spectre of Simon and Garfunkel. The work on the album is substantial, proving beyond doubt that Simon's reliance on Garfunkel was minimal. 'Peace Like A River' recalls 'The Only Living Boy in New York', but can now be appreciated as a trailer for 'American Tune' the following year. It charts the disillusionment of the 60s' activists, now bound and gagged but still optimistic, like Simon, about a brighter future. 'Everything Put Together Falls Apart' was a convenient title for critics, who interpreted it as a reflection on the split, but the main reason for its inception was Simon's desire to open a song with 'paraphernalia', a word whch he proudly noted was rarely heard in pop songs on AM radio! 'Armistice Day' had been knocking around since 1968 and had begun life as an overtly anti-Vietnam piece, but by the time he came to record it the song had metamorphosed into a strange, reliant love song and a paean to lost idealism. 'Papa Hobo' is another weary road song, but is strongly imbued with a first-hand impression of the 'Detroit perfume' of Motor City USA. The automotive dream has proved to be an illusion and the road is now the escape – not the homesick return journey of 'Homeward Bound', but the way out to an uncertain future.

If comparisons were to be made with the halcyon days of Simon and Garfunkel, they were saved for the album's last track, 'Congratulations', (which borrowed from Little Anthony and the Imperials' tearjerker 'Tears On My Pillow'); a lush piano ballad – played by Larry Knechtel who had performed a similar task on 'Bridge Over Troubled Water' – which found Simon wistfully reflecting on the frailty of relationships. Gone is the healing, soothing possibility of the song's protagonist being a bridge; here Simon maturely addresses an audience which has grown up. The first flush of innocent, lost love – also tackled in 'America' and 'Duncan' – is now replaced by a sombre consideration of whether a man and a woman can ever live together in peace. Simon notices the courtrooms full of couples awaiting divorce, and would indeed find himself waiting in line there a few years later in 1975 when he and Peggy were divorced.

As an album *Paul Simon* was a vindication: proof that Simon could function creatively away from the monster that Simon and Garfunkel had become. Its sales amounted to about a tenth of those of *Bridge Over Troubled Water*, but the reviews were respectful and 'Mother and Child Reunion' and 'Me and Julio . . .' were hit singles in both Britain and America. One album and two hit singles couldn't hope to vanquish Simon and Garfunkel's memory, but it was a start. While he was not prepared to tour to help promote the album, Simon reluctantly submitted himself for interviews, fending off the inevitable reunion questions and quietly and cogently talking critics through his album. Courteous and composed, confident about his new release, Paul Simon seemed set to face the future on his own terms.

Simon's label, however, were not so sanguine. It is record company policy that when a successful act splits up or starts to fade, a 'Greatest Hits' album is rushed out to capitalize on their fans' devotion. No 'new' Simon and Garfunkel album could be concocted from out-takes or unreleased songs, so CBS weren't slow off the mark with *Simon and Garfunkel's Greatest Hits*, which was released only a few months after Simon's eagerly anticipated solo album. For once, it was an effective compilation; rather than relying upon already available versions of the duo's most familiar songs, live versions of 'For Emily, Whenever I May Find Her', 'Feelin' Groovy', 'Homeward Bound' and 'Kathy's Song' were included, and gave a reminder of how powerful the two men could be in concert. The obvious move would have been a live Simon and Garfunkel album, and in fact a concert at Tufts University in 1966 was recorded and scheduled, but it was never released although it was widely bootlegged. It gives the listener an opportunity to hear such familiar songs as 'The Dangling Conversation' and 'A Poem On the Underground Wall' performed away from the studio, and demonstrates again the strength of the duo's harmonies on familiar material; it also includes the otherwise unavailable 'Red Rubber Ball'.

As for bootlegs, Simon's songwriting was so painstaking and unprolific that virtually everything he wrote ended up on an official album. *Chez*, a tape Simon recorded in New York for Kathy in London in 1965, is mainly guitar instrumentals or songs he had already recorded for his *Songbook*. Live bootlegs were interesting only as souvenirs of the concerts, such as those they performed at the peak of their career, but Simon and Garfunkel usually stuck to their best-known songs. There is, however, an extra verse of 'The Boxer' to be found on bootleg, which first appeared legitimately on 1974's *Live Rhymin'*. In concert the duo would also sometimes include a couple of Everly Brothers tunes, one regular favourite being a version of Gene Autry's maudlin 1931 hit, 'That Silver Haired Daddy Of Mine', which the Everlys had recorded. I remember 1970 at the Royal Albert Hall and the incongruity of these two 'serious' young men happily wallowing in that classic piece of country and western sentimentality. Both men were aware of their 'serious' image and were occasionally tempted to release albums with titles like *So Young, Yet So Full Of Pain*!

The *Greatest Hits* album was rushed out in June 1972 to coincide with a one-off Simon and Garfunkel reunion. Warren Beatty was working with Senator George McGovern's campaign against Nixon and capitalized on his wealth of showbiz contacts to organize a number of benefit shows, the biggest of which was a concert at New York's Madison Square Garden. It was an event which brought together a number of acts who had long ceased working together, including Mike Nichols and Elaine May, Peter, Paul and Mary, and Simon and Garfunkel. A politician with impeccable liberal credentials, McGovern was a concerned Democrat determined to bring the Vietnam war to a swift conclusion and offer an alternative to the innate conservatism of a second Nixon term. The pair appeared to a rapturous reception and ran through a selection of ten Simon and Garfunkel hits as well as a solo Simon version of 'Mother and Child Reunion'. McGovern's bid for the presidency was obviously an important enough issue for the two men temporarily to set aside their differences, but the set was not a success, since the duo were just going through the motions; it certainly didn't lay the foundations for a lasting reunion. *Rolling Stone* noted: 'They stood at their mikes looking straight ahead, like two commuters clutching adjacent straps on the morning train!' Despite the help of Warren Beatty and Simon and Garfunkel, though, McGovern was swept away by a Nixon landslide in November.

Early in 1973 Simon obviously felt confident enough of his own new work to allow himself the luxury of reflecting on his past. *The Songs of Paul Simon* was a lavishly produced book which contained every song Simon had written since 1963 except for three that he couldn't get permission to republish and 'two really bad ones I wouldn't want to look at'. Simon's introduction to the book provides a fascinating glimpse into his creative processes as it charts the progress of his songwriting, starting with the simple act of picking up a guitar and playing: 'Once I pick a key and start to play, I sing any words that come into my head without trying to make any sense out of them. I tend to sing easy words with a concentration of 'oohs' and 'ah' sounds which are musically pleasing to me. I also like words beginning with g's and l's and words that have t's and k's in them. Sometimes during this stream of consciousness singing a phrase will develop that has a naturalness and a meaning, in which case I keep it and start to build a song around it.' Simon ended on a note which recalled his sleeve notes on the very first solo album eight years before: 'I think my next songs will be better.'

There was soon an opportunity to find out since *There Goes Rhymin' Simon* came out in May 1973. Considering the delays inherent in his style of writing and recording, a new Paul Simon album in just over a year was quick going, as he told Lorraine Alterman: 'An album in less than eighteen months for me is lightning!' As its title implies, *Rhymin' Simon* is a lighter work than Simon's others to date. Even the cover has a kind of endearing naïvety to it which Simon and Garfunkel would never have sanctioned, illustrating Paul Simon's life from the teenage DA character in the top right-hand corner to the proud father cradling his son Harper at bottom left. Evidence of the wheel coming full circle was also apparent in the songs themselves: 'Was A Sunny Day' in part recalled his Tom and Jerry days, the chorus was lifted from the Cadillacs' 1955 hit 'Speedoo', while 'American Tune' was a deft evocation of America at the time of Watergate which could stand firmly alongside the very best of Simon and Garfunkel.

'American Tune' looms large over the album. It is a rueful reflection on the betrayal of the nation by the chicaneries of Nixon's White House. Simon had inherited his parents' scepticism of that sly politician: 'Nixon was always the villain in my parents' eyes. He was the guy who would not play fair and be vindictive.' Even from that darkest hour, though, Simon summons up a ray of hope and focuses on the Statue of Liberty as a beacon towering over the New York skyline, viewing it with the same sense of awe and promise that those early immigrants crowding onto Ellis Island must have done. It is in the final verse that Simon's genius bubbles over as he devoutly sings: *'We come on the ship they call the Mayflower/We come on the ship that sailed the moon/We come in the age's most uncertain hour/And sing an American tune'*.

From the Pilgrim Fathers to the landing of the Eagle on the moon, Simon imbues the song with a real sense of national pride, but carefully avoids blatant muscle-flexing patriotism which would have made the song unpalatable. While the song is populated by shattered dreams, uneasy friendships and battered souls, there is a residual glimmer of hope and optimism. Removed from the clearing where 'The Boxer' defiantly stood, here Simon's newly panoramic scope embraces the whole nation at its most precarious, post-war moment. Simon was particularly proud when *Rolling Stone* voted 'American Tune' Song of the Year for 1973, but was careful to point out that the beautiful melody was not his, but came from Bach's 'Sacred Heart' section of the *St Matthew Passion*. 'American Tune' virtually became an alternative national anthem and it was this song Paul Simon chose to play at President Carter's Inaugural Ball in 1977. Almost ten years later it was heard all round the world during the 100th birthday celebrations for the Statue of Liberty in 1986.

Rhymin' Simon was his most cohesive album to date. A refreshing lightness of touch had come to Simon's work which did not in any way lessen his stature as a major songwriter; quite the reverse in fact. The newly found deftness signified a spontaneity which Simon never again matched. Here were a sense of fun which wasn't forced, pensive reflections on the state of the nation, mature recognition of his own fallibility, breezy pop songs and a proud parent's song for his newly born son. Simon delighted in the first line of 'Kodachrome' – *'When I think back on all the crap I learned in high school . . .'* – but US radio stations took offence over 'crap', while the BBC reasoned that 'Kodachrome' was advertising! In fact, the song had begun life as a tune called 'Going Home', but

Simon felt that subject had been done to death and tried to approach the subject from left of centre.

'Take Me To The Mardi Gras' captures all the colour and atmosphere of New Orleans at carnival time, and Reverend Juter's falsetto is a joy. 'Saint Judy's Comet' is an enchanting lullaby, delightfully self-mocking in the lines: *'If I can't sing my boy to sleep/Well it makes your famous daddy look so dumb'*. Simon was asked by *Playboy* years later why he didn't write more songs about his son: 'I tried to, but I was just too overcome with love to write. I couldn't think of anything to write other than, "You totally amaze and mesmerize me, I'm so in love with you I can't contain myself", and that just didn't seem like a healthy song to write.' 'Was A Sunny Day' features harmonies from the Roche sisters who had studied with Simon in 1971 and went on to a career as artists in their own right, releasing three albums on WEA in the 1980s. The song has a charming summery feel, with the soul-saving rock and roll music pouring from the radio. The album's last track, 'Loves Me Like A Rock', is a joyous, celebratory slab of Gospel, while 'Something So Right' is one of Simon's most beautiful melodies but is spoilt lyrically by the uncharacteristically clumsy analogy between his emotional state and the Great Wall of China! 'Tenderness', a lovely, lilting, wistful ballad, has him pointedly searching for some *'tenderness beneath your honesty'*.

So impressed had Simon been by the Staple Singers' hit, 'I'll Take You There', that he decided to try out the same musicians and studio to see if he could recapture some of that atmosphere. He and his engineer Phil Ramone were so pleased with the legendary Muscle Shoals studio that they ended up recording half the album there. The gospel harmony group the Dixie Hummingbirds were also featured, and the Onward Brass Band were used to create the effect of New Orleans at Mardi Gras time.

Musically the album has many diverse and fascinating strands, which again display Simon's ability to integrate wth all manner of different musical idioms and gain an effect that is uniquely and unmistakably his own. The musical odyssey he had embarked on with *Paul Simon* lay here at the very core of his album. It was the first full flowering of a pioneering spirit which would colour Simon's whole career and lead to the *Graceland* phenomenon more than a decade later. The album gave Paul Simon a Top 10 hit in Britain with 'Take Me To The Mardi Gras', while 'Kodachrome' and 'Loves Me Like A Rock' were massive hits in America.

Simon is very selective about his work for other performers, but once he chooses to help he is generous with both time and trouble. Aside from taking them on tour in 1973, Simon produced the Urubamba album. He also worked with the Roche sisters on their debut album, *Seductive Reasoning*, in 1975 after his lawyer had helped the sisters land their CBS contract. In 1973 Simon donated an otherwise unavailable song of his own called 'Groundhog' to Peter Yarrow's album *That's Enough For Me* – his solo debut after years with Peter, Paul and Mary. 'Groundhog' is a wry song which follows on from 'Papa Hobo' (*'livin' a hobo's life is not the glamor that it seems'*) and notes that *'even the leader of the band/gets the blues when he's alone'*. Simon was gratified to be approached by Leonard Bernstein and asked to contribute some lyrics to Bernstein's *Mass* which was being composed as the première work for New York's John F. Kennedy Center For The Performing Arts. Bernstein had become quite an advocate of rock 'poetry' in the late 60s, and was particularly enamoured of Simon's work. Simon's contribution pithily ran: *'Half the people are stoned and the other half are waiting for the next election/Half the people are drowned and the other half are swimming in the wrong direction'*. It was a quatrain in the mood of 'American Tune', which captured the essence of Fortress America at the beginning of the 70s.

The years between *Bridge Over Troubled Water* and *Rhymin' Simon* had seen Simon develop as a writer and mature as a person. He had studied classical guitar and now listened to more diverse forms of music – Antonio Carlos Jobim and Gospel in particular had a lasting effect on his music. Jobim was a profound influence on his use of the scale in the *Still Crazy After All These Years* album in 1975, while Simon responded instinctively to the gospel fervour of the Staple Singers and the Dixie Hummingbirds because it recalled the doo-wop music he so loved to hear on the radio in New York in the 1950s. That broadening of his musical horizons and his own growing confidence in his new material persuaded Simon to tour in 1973 to promote his new album.

As with every facet of his professional career, Simon planned the tour with extreme care and caution. The hand-picked band which accompanied Simon on tour in America and Europe throughout 1973 was augmented by the Gospel group the Jessy Dixon Singers and the Latin American musicians Urubamba (who featured two former members of Los Incas), whose own album Simon had produced that year. The shows were a triumph, with Simon delving into his own repertoire and confident enough to encourage comparisons with Simon and Garfunkel. The Gospel influence was there to bolster 'Bridge Over Troubled Water' and 'The Sound of Silence', while Simon's solo versions of 'Homeward Bound' and 'America' were touching and resilient.

Live Rhymin', the 1974 album of the tour, displayed Simon's inventiveness as a guitarist – a skill which has been consistently overlooked – and the audience's delight at witnessing Simon in the flesh was obvious. At the end of the album someone calls out for him to say a few words: 'Well', says Simon, rock poet and spokesman for his generation, 'let's hope we continue to live . . .!' The audience acknowledge his wisdom, the sage has spoken! The same thing happened at the Graceland Concerts at the Royal Albert Hall in 1987 – a call came from high in the gallery that Simon should say something, and without missing a beat he deliberately repeated his exact words from *Live Rhymin'*!

What is so uplifting about *Live Rhymin'* is Simon's willingness to reinvest his songs with fresh and imaginative musical settings, largely thanks to the Gospel of the Jessy Dixon Singers, who manage to lay the ghost of 'Bridge Over Troubled Water' by taking it back to its Gospel roots, affirming its strength as a song even when stripped of Garfunkel's reverential approach and the lush orchestration, and forsaking the all too familiar piano introduction. At last Simon was centre-stage, singing his best-known song, not watching from the wings. The Jessy Dixon Singers' backing on 'The Sound of Silence' perforce robs the song of its isolation, but gives it a new spectral dimension, which Simon's slow, bluesy vocal enhances. The album offers Simon the opportunity to repossess the best of his own work, and to infuse it with musical styles which fascinated him at that stage of his career. The thorny problem of just how Simon could tackle chestnuts such as 'America', and particularly 'Homeward Bound' after so many years is a problem which faces every performer at some time. The audience's nostalgia for a familiar bedrock of old tunes contrasts with the artist's desire to acquaint them with what he considers the best of his new work. In 1986 Simon spoke to David Fricke about that dilemma, admitting that 'Homeward Bound' was one song he found particularly frustrating to keep singing: 'Then I thought . . . "The mistake you're making is you act as if this is a representation of your work now, instead of a representation of you when you were twenty-three years old. Think of this as a photo of you at twenty-three up in a railroad station in Liverpool, then it's not so bad".'

Simon felt that to tour and release a live album was in a sense an obligation and that it offered an audience the opportunity 'to keep a sense of continuity'. With the release of *Live Rhymin*' Paul Simon fulfilled that obligation. He spoke to *Melody Maker* about the tour in 1973: 'I just decided to do something so I'd be getting off my ass. . . . I'll go out and I'll sing my songs and I'll try and sing in tune, and basically that's what I have to offer. People either want to hear me sing my songs or they don't, so I feel that nobody will be expecting any more of me than that.'

With such statements, it seemed that Simon was hitting his mid-thirties in a happier, more relaxed state of mind. The challenge he had forced himself to meet on the split of Simon and Garfunkel had been met; with three solo albums under his belt he had earned the right to be taken on his own terms. The constant royalties from his songs kept the wolf from his well-appointed door – his songs have been covered by a staggeringly diverse array of artists including Frank Sinatra, Aretha Franklin, Cliff Richard, Elvis Presley, the Paul Butterfield Blues Band, Andy Williams, Stevie Wonder, Yes, Willie Nelson; even polemical 80s' folkie Billy Bragg, who later went on record condemning Simon's Graceland project, utilized the opening lines of 'The Leaves That Are Green' for his own 'A New England'.

Since *Bookends*, Simon's standing in the rock world had been high, but such was the enduring strength of his songs that he was hailed as an influential figure well into the 80s. Vince Clarke, co-founder of Depeche Mode and Yazoo, the epitome of synthesizer wizard and new pop star – he wrote the classic 'Only You' – admitted in 1987 that the one person he'd like to work with was Paul Simon, while Nick Laird-Clowes, leader of the promising British band Dream Academy, was a Simon fan of long standing, and Simon at one time looked set to produce the trio's debut album. Suzanne Vega's 1987 hit 'Luka' bore a passing resemblance to 'A Most Peculiar Man', while her contemporary Michelle Shocked cited Simon as a seminal influence in a 1987 interview, where she praised his 'right-on politics' and later recorded his 'Stranded In A Limousine'. Simon's influence was also cited by the Bangles when they named 'The Only Living Boy In New York' as one of their all-time favourite songs. The oddest tribute, though, came with a 1986 album *Dig?* by the Georgia band, the Coolies, whose debut consisted solely of Paul Simon songs covered in a rather unorthodox fashion. Lacking the charm of Big Daddy – who among other things Ricky Nelsonized Bruce Springsteen's 'Dancing In The Dark' – the Coolies crashed into Simon and Garfunkel classics head-on: 'Bridge Over Troubled Water' was a

Heavy Metal thrash, while 'Mrs Robinson' was an instrumental à la Ventures!

Riches and fulsome testimonials, however, did not ensure happiness, and for Simon 1975 was a watershed. His relationship with CBS was disharmonious, and while recording his new album, Paul and Peggy Simon were divorced, with Paul retaining access to their only son, three-year-old Harper James. It was one of life's ironies, which Simon could not help but observe, that here he was, a rich, talented young man in the prime of life, adored and admired by millions, yet unable to keep his own marriage together, and he spoke of his own sense of 'worthlessness' at this time.

Channelling his energies into his work was one way of easing the tension; re-opening tentative lines of communication with Art Garfunkel was another. Quite *why* the world was so keen on a Simon and Garfunkel reunion is curious. From the outset it was obvious that the bias in the partnership was towards Simon, and his solo work was indubitably stronger than anything Garfunkel could produce alone. It was more to do with the two men being on stage together again which gave audiences a chance to reflect on what had been, and that – as Simon sang in 'The Boxer's' 'missing' verse – '*after changes upon changes we are more or less the same*'. That is what people *wanted* to believe: that the idealism and optimism of the 60s hadn't ended up down a dead end street.

In the mid-70s, rock and roll had become a bloated artifice, bands ploughed lucratively round stadiums delivering bombastic but ultimately hollow spectacles; there was a craving for the sort of intimacy which Simon and Garfunkel had once offered. By 1975 it was apparent that the Beatles would never get together again, and Simon and Garfunkel were one of the few icons of the Golden Age willing to bite the bullet and reform. Already the 60s were taking on a Wordsworthian aspect: 'Bliss was it in that dawn to be alive/But to be young was very heaven'. The cosy glow of nostalgia had seeped into the 70s, which had thrown up few new heroes of its own; the children of the Woodstock generation were gratefully accepting the idols of their parents until the real thing came along! The idea of Simon and Garfunkel getting together again offered security and encouragement that things could get better, could return again to the 'blissful' dawn of youth. Like many vestiges of 60s' idealism, it proved to be illusory.

With Garfunkel exploiting the commercial lushness of the partnership, his albums had been steady sellers, though critics were constantly bemoaning the lack of bite. Simon decided to give his former partner that edge. 'My Little Town' was written specifically for Art, a 'nasty' lyric for him to get his teeth into. Simon told Bill Flanagan that the song 'was purely an act of imagination, as opposed to autobiography. There's no element of me in there at all.' The fact that there is none of Paul Simon in the coiled malevolence of the song makes it an even more remarkable achievement. It is as fine a depiction as any the rock culture has produced of the strains and strictures of growing up in a claustrophobic small town while bursting to get out. Simon deftly paints the scenario, saving the best till last: '*I never meant nothin'/I was just my father's son. . . . Twitching like a finger/On the trigger of a gun*'. A crystal-sharp image of the boy's status, harnessed in the town which has so little to offer, taut and capable of violence. The song saw the duo recording together again for the first time in five years and CBS, keen to capitalize on the rapprochement, included 'My Little Town' on both Simon and Garfunkel's 1975 solo albums.

Another project which occupied Simon during late 1974 and early 1975 was the scoring of a film soundtrack, his first since *The Graduate*. Simon's choice of Warren Beatty's *Shampoo* was an understandable one; he had known Beatty since their work together on the McGovern campaign three years before, and the film's wholeheartedly liberal sentiments struck a responsive chord in Simon as the film railed against Nixon's election in 1968. On paper, *Shampoo* had everything going for it, but on film it was a disaster. Beatty remains one of Hollywood's most bankable and articulate stars; director Hal Ashby had hit with the anti-establishment but commercially viable *The Last Detail* starring Jack Nicholson, and scriptwriter Robert Towne was a hot property following his Oscar-winning script for *Chinatown*. Those ingredients, plus Julie Christie and Goldie Hawn, with Paul Simon's first motion picture score in nearly ten years, *had* to be a winning package. But, as so often with 'winning packages' in Hollywood, it wasn't! As scriptwriter William Goldman wrote, in the movies 'nobody knows anything!'

The film could have been a powerful exposition on the nature of Nixon's politics in the aftermath of the Watergate revelations. Instead, through the rosy hue of nostalgia, it centred on events in the late 60s with a suitably evocative soundtrack from the Beatles, Buffalo Springfield et al., and Simon's contribution was negligible. There were odd snatches of someone humming and gently strumming an acoustic guitar, but they were so minimal as to be wholly redundant. Simon originally intended 'Have A Good Time' and 'Silent Eyes' for the film, but neither were used; rewritten, they appeared on his next album.

While Simon had been at pains throughout his career to point out that his songs were rarely autobiographical, the sentiments throughout *Still Crazy After All These Years* could not but help reflect his recent divorce from Peggy. He told a journalist at the time: 'The whole album *is* about my marriage. . . . "I Do It For Your Love" got it out of me – that was a very emotional song for me, a very truthful song. I was *crying* in the middle of that song, when I was writing some of those lyrics. That's really me – I don't know how good a song it is, but it's really about my life. . . . I think that's what I write best about, men and women. But I hardly *ever* write about them romantically. In fact, the romantic songs that I wrote are the ones that I dislike the most – "For Emily," all that stuff, I just can't stand it.'

The album was the smoothest sounding of Simon's solo work to date. While it lacked the musical eclecticism of *Rhymin' Simon*, *Still Crazy* has a jazzier feel, largely due to the friends Simon thanked on the album sleeve. Chuck Israels and David Sorin Collyer were two jazzmen in New York under whom Simon studied composition and arrangement while writing songs for the album. It was the musicians on the *Still Crazy* album – Steve Gadd, Richard Tee, Tony Levin – who formed the nucleus of Simon's band for the next few years, and who appeared with him in his *One Trick Pony* film in 1980.

Still Crazy After All These Years (released in 1975) was a mature album for an audience which had grown up alongside Simon; the prissily poetic isolation of the early Simon and Garfunkel years was now replaced by a sense of domesticity and loss. It was to these ageing hippies that Simon now addressed his work: 'People thirty years old wonder why they're not getting off on popular music the way they once did, and it's because nobody's singing for them', Simon told Timothy White in *Crawdaddy*. 'When you reach a certain age you're not naïve anymore. Everything I write can't be a philosophical truth, but it certainly isn't innocent, because I'm not. Music is for ever. Music should grow and mature with you, following you right up until you die.' With the new sense of perspective born of a broken marriage and a much loved son, and with his adolescence half a lifetime away, Paul Simon's new songs were a reflection of where he and many of his generation now stood as he reached a crossroads of his life and art. The album's title track is a good example of this, particularly the final verse with the resonant line, '*But I would not be convicted by a jury of my peers*'. That final verse also contains a hint of the coiled violence inherent in 'My Little Town', as Simon fears '*I'll do some damage one fine day*'.

The album is reminiscent of a Woody Allen film – the neuroses of a prosperous, painfully self-aware New York Jew, who can only learn to understand himself by turning inward and exposing the results. Take 'You're Kind', a brittle love song about failed romance. The break-up is attributed to the fact that: '*I like to sleep with the window open/And you keep the window closed. . . .*' It was a song whose lyrics fascinated the composer; years later he recalled it to Bill Flanagan: 'It's an indifferent song: someone treats you really nice and you say I'm leaving! You could either say it was for an arbitrary reason (I like to sleep with the window open and you sleep with the window closed). Or you could say it was a metaphor for freedom. It works either way. . . .'

'I Do It For Your Love' is another song on a similar theme, delineating the breakdown of a marriage, like 'Overs' from *Bookends*, but full of touching, romantic moments before the fall – sharing colds, rummaging in junk shops – before the oblique, opaque final verse, '*The sting of reason, the splash of tears/The northern and southern hemispheres/Love emerges and it disappears*'.

'50 Ways To Leave Your Lover' gave Simon his first US Number 1 since 'Bridge Over Troubled Water', which is ironic considering the song originally came about as a novelty sequence of rhymes thought up to amuse his son Harper. It's one of the few pop hits where the chorus is actually weaker than the verses, and it brings to mind David Bowie's 'Starman' which is similarly unbalanced. Simon had another US hit with 'Gone At Last', which was originally intended as a duet with Bette Midler; however, complications arose and Simon eventually dueted devastatingly with Phoebe Snow.

'Silent Eyes' was an enigmatic conclusion to the album; chillingly sung, it stands as a curious avowal of faith from a determined agnostic. 'Have A Good Time' finds Simon with '*one more year on the line*'; he is in skittish humour, and like Chuck Berry on 'Back In The USA', he delights at being born in America with such a high standard of living to be enjoyed. The rancour of 'American Tune' is a long way behind.

The inscrutable 'Night Game' deals with Simon's other great love in life – baseball. Once asked by *Rolling Stone* what he would have been if he hadn't had a career as a successful songwriter and performer, Simon replied without hesitation 'a relief pitcher'.

Simon was a dyed-in-the-wool New York Yankees fan, and Joe DiMaggio and Mickey Mantle were as much heroes of his as John Cheever and Elvis Presley. He had been given the honour of throwing the opening ball of the 1970 World Series, and even proposed to his second wife Carrie Fisher after a Yankees game. 'I always get very calm with baseball,' Simon once said. 'Night Game' deals with a pitcher's death and the ritualistic elements of his funeral. Simon recalled writing the song because of his fascination not only with baseball itself but also with the circus element of modern sport which recalls the gladiatorial combats of Roman times.

Still Crazy won Simon another handful of Grammys – a fact which he modestly attributed to Stevie Wonder not releasing an album that year! It saw him once again hitting a home run, and it was to be his last album for five years. 1975 was a busy year for Simon, who once again toured to promote the album. The Jessy Dixon Singers again lent Gospel fervour to the new material from the *Still Crazy* album, and also in the band was veteran harmonica player Toots Thielmans, who Simon obviously relished sharing the stage with. Simon's brother Eddie was running New York's Guitar Study Centre, where his elder brother hosted a seminar in early 1975, discussing his playing and the development of 'American Tune'. Simon also appeared several times, including one stint as guest host, on the massively popular *Saturday Night Live* TV show; the nearest American TV came to the freewheeling satire of the BBC during the late 60s.

A whole new breed of stars, including Chevy Chase, Dan Aykroyd, John Belushi, and Gilda Radner, were introduced on *Saturday Night Live*; but the show's mastermind was its producer Lorne Michaels, who remains one of Simon's closest friends. In September 1975, Simon and Garfunkel appeared on the show together, achieving one of the highest ratings of the series. The pair played their reunion for laughs, milking the event for all it was worth. Simon greeted his erstwhile partner with, 'So you've come crawling back!' Another guest on the show that night was Randy Newman, the cult singer-songwriter whose rueful songs have been compared to Simon's. In 1964, while Simon was tackling 'major works' such as 'The Sound Of Silence', Newman was scoring the drag racing drama *The Lively Set*, but he soon developed his own idiosyncratic style. Simon later appeared as guest vocalist on Newman's song 'The Blues' from his 1983 *Trouble In Paradise* album; Newman has since cited that song as the only one he regrets having written! 'It sorta makes fun of the mock-sensitive song-writer, like Simon was, and clones of him still are', Newman said in a 1987 interview.

Another *Saturday Night Live* special in 1975 featured Paul Simon playing alongside George Harrison, joining the former Beatle on guitar for 'Here Comes The Sun'. Indeed, such was the power and popularity of *Saturday Night Live* that rumour has it that the only time all four Beatles ever considered reforming was for a spoof slot on the show. Simon was a guest at Lorne Michaels' wedding in 1981, and witnessing the state of John Belushi beforehand, cleaned him up and shaved him to make him presentable for the ceremony.

Simon admitted during the *Still Crazy* tour that he felt most comfortable playing seated venues of 7,000 to 8,000 people, but he delivered a stunning show at the smaller London Palladium at the tour's conclusion in December 1975. Only weeks before, however, a few hundred yards away from Simon's venue, the Sex Pistols had made their debut and ensured that rock and roll would never be the same again. Simon told Chris Charlesworth of *Melody Maker* at that time: 'I don't think I'm going to start work on another album. I think I'm going to do something else . . . a show, a movie. Rather than write ten songs and sing them, I'll try and write my songs *for* something.'

It was a portentous statement. Paul Simon ducked below the parapet for five years following the release of *Still Crazy*. Like John Lennon, who 'disappeared' at the same time, he felt there had to be some alternative to the vacuous treadmill of tour-album-tour-album on which he found himself. While rock music underwent its most significant change since the emergence of the Beatles, Paul Simon's voice was silent.

Think Too Much

For the last half of the 1970s, Paul Simon was barely visible. As one of the most eloquent commentators of the 1960s, his absence was noted. He made sporadic guest appearances – on saxophonist David Sanborn's 1976 debut album, for example – and continued to make occasional appearances on *Saturday Night Live* with friends Charles Grodin and Chevy Chase. He also guested on a Lily Tomlin TV Special and played a benefit concert in May 1976 for the New York public libraries. His recording work was limited to a competent cover of Sam Cooke's 'Wonderful World' which was a US hit in 1978 for Simon, Garfunkel and Taylor (James). But a bloody musical revolution was underway and the Punks storming the Winter Palace of the rock establishment had little time for the likes of cosy, complacent Paul Simon; conversely Simon had little in common with the shrieking anarchy of the Sex Pistols, although he did check out gigs by Bruce Springsteen, the B-52s and the Clash – 'but I had to leave to protect my ears'. The thrust of Punk was aimed at the cherished and venerable foundations of rock music. In Punk's tumult there was little room for the subtlety and craftsmanship of a Paul Simon. Punk performed an essential service in clearing rock's clogged arteries, but it was a short-lived coup and its aftermath saw the status quo quickly returned.

Viewing his long-term future, Simon was keen to make a move into film, and with the expiry of his CBS contract looming he felt a switch to Warner Bros, with their sizeable film arm, would be a positive step. CBS, though, were obviously not keen to lose one of their major acts; while Paul Simon's sales as a solo artist never approached those of Simon and Garfunkel, he was still a steady and reliable seller, and his presence on the label lent kudos to CBS. One way in which Simon – who owed CBS one more album – tried to ease himself off the label was with a proposal that he should duet with labelmates on an album of covers; James Taylor, Billy Joel and

Bruce Springsteen were among those approached, but the nightmare logistics of contractual ties led to the project being shelved. Instead, amidst considerable acrimony, a solo 'Greatest Hits' package was released in 1977, exonerating Simon from his legal obligations. In fact, *Greatest Hits Etc* is a strong compilation, collecting all the best examples of Simon's solo work, including an otherwise unavailable version of 'American Tune'.

The two new songs on the album were released as singles during 1977 and provided Simon with minor American hits. 'Slip Slidin' Away' was a taut, compelling song, aided and abetted by the tasteful country and western harmonies of the Oak Ridge Boys. The song's beguiling melody belies the bitterness of the lyric which attacks the comfort of illusion – '*We . . . believe we're gliding down the highway/When in fact we're slip, slidin' away*'. The idea that we draw nearer our dreams as we get older is denied by Simon. The penultimate verse is touchingly autobiographical with Simon as the single parent separated from his only son. 'Stranded In A Limousine' is an altogether funkier exercise, a jazzy detour onto New York's mean streets, concerning a mobster who left the neighbourhood '*like a rattlesnake sheds its skin*'.

The *One Trick Pony* project was one which constantly occupied Simon towards the end of the 70s. Disillusioned by his previous abortive film soundtracks, he felt it was time fully to immerse himself in an original film. To test the water, Simon appeared as the vapid Tony Lacey in Woody Allen's Oscar-winning 1977 film *Annie Hall*. In a neat piece of casting against type, Tony Lacey is a born again Californian, bemoaning the fact that in New York, if you want to see a movie you have to stand in line and – sin of sins – it might be raining! Living in Charlie Chaplin's old house means nothing to Tony Lacey – Nelson Eddy has lived there before. Although his part was little more than a cameo in a film laden with cameos, Simon was confident and convincing as a vacuous LA parasite.

While filming *Annie Hall*, Simon enjoyed a relationship with Shelley Duvall, who appeared in the film as the sort of rock critic Simon most dreaded in real life; but by 1978 Simon had begun dating actress Carrie Fisher. The couple's relationship was on and off over the next five years, until finally they married in August 1983, when Carrie was twenty-seven and Paul was forty-two. Carrie came from a showbiz family; her parents, Debbie Reynolds and singer Eddie Fisher, were Hollywood royalty, but in 1959, when Carrie was three, they were divorced under the scorching glare of the public gaze and Fisher went off to marry Elizabeth Taylor. Carrie had been performing since she was twelve and made her film debut as the nymphet in *Shampoo*. Worldwide fame came to her in 1977 when she starred as Princess Leia in *Star Wars*. Her relationship with Simon was tempestuous and their marriage lasted less than a year, during which time she tragically miscarried their child. Of the split in April 1984, Simon said there was 'no animosity'.

In 1980 Simon told Ray Coleman: 'Several myths surround me, and one is that I'm a recluse, never leave my home in New York, write miserable songs and don't smile. I'm not sad at all, although everyone is depressed at sometime in their life. I go out and meet people and smile!' His stints on *Saturday Night Live* were indicative of Simon's laconic sense of humour. In one sketch he appeared as a guest denied entrance to a restaurant because he's too short, and in another he clumped around in a turkey suit alongside Elliot Gould. In 1978 Simon appeared as himself in Eric Idle's painstakingly accurate Beatles film spoof, *The Rutles*. Interviewed alongside Mick Jagger, Simon deadpanned about 'the Pre-Fab Four' and emphatically denied that the Rutles had influenced his work in any way whatsoever! A few years later Simon guested in a Steve Martin video, eager to pick up hints on songwriting, only to be admonished by Martin with, 'Not now Paul, I'm talking about comedy technique, songwriting comes later.'

These were all appetizers; the main course would be the 1980s' film and album, *One Trick Pony*. His novel indefinitely postponed, Simon applied himself to the craft of screenwriting. He explained to Dave Marsh in 1980: 'I wanted to do something other than just record an album. I felt my choices were either to write a Broadway show or a movie. I chose the movie because I thought it would be closer to the process of recording. You get a take, and that's your take. I don't have to go in every night to see whether the cast is performing. Also, I could still record and use the music as a score. But if I'd written a show, I couldn't have recorded my own stuff – other people would have to sing it.'

The choice of an actor to play the central character, Jonah Levin, caused problems. Simon's acting experience was limited, and Warner were unsure whether he could carry the part through an entire movie, but Warner's commitment to the project rested on Simon's involvement. Gary Busey, who had scored such a hit in the title role of *The Buddy Holly Story*, was considered, and Simon also broached the idea with Academy Award winner Richard Dreyfuss – who had coincidentally made an early appearance in *The Graduate*. A known fan of Simon's, Dreyfuss was quoted in 1977 as saying: 'I always knew that I could be a star for a whole audience that didn't relate to John Wayne or Al Pacino. An urban, progressive, intellectually oriented audience . . . people who listen to Paul Simon and Randy Newman.' But after consideration, Simon dismissed the idea: 'There was no way that Dreyfuss could be in the movie and open his mouth and have my voice come out.'

The challenge of writing an original screenplay, scoring and starring in a feature-length film, was a personal Everest for Simon; a challenge was needed and creating an authentic rock film provided it. Dylan's rambling four-hour *Renaldo & Clara* of 1978 had won few converts; rock films were still largely quickie exploitation vehicles or lavishly self-indulgent exercises. Many still regarded 1956's *The Girl Can't Help It* as *the* rock and roll movie, and twenty years on little had changed.

By the time Simon tackled *One Trick Pony*, promo videos had yet to register fully on the rock scene, and a film seemed the best medium to communicate Simon's views on the industry in which he had excelled for nearly two decades. The success of 1969's *Easy Rider* had spawned hundreds of imitators, and the counter culture, for a while, became marketable in Hollywood's eyes. Above-average efforts like *Alice's Restaurant* and *Taking Off* were opportunities for parents to try and understand their errant children. Otherwise, concert films with obligatory fantasy sequences were the norm (*Abba: The Movie*, Led Zeppelin's *The Song Remains The Same*, T.Rex's *Born To Boogie*). There were some straightforward documentaries which provided a fascinating insight into life on the road, like Dylan's *Don't Look Back* and the Stones' *Gimme Shelter*, which were exemplary. The overwhelming global success of 1977's *Saturday Night Fever* (the soundtrack of which eclipsed the sales of *Bridge Over Troubled Water*) set the pace for rock films at the end of the 70s. The nemesis of this genre was reached by the film *Sgt. Pepper's Lonely Hearts Club Band* in 1978; Hollywood reasoned that a box office smash must result from having Beatles' songs sung by the Bee Gees, who had written the *Saturday Night Fever* soundtrack and could do no wrong at the time. But Beatles, Bee Gees and every other sort of fan stayed away in droves. There had been all too few lucid and revealing films of the rock lifestyle. *One Trick Pony* effectively changed that.

Simon was aware of the enormous responsibility resting on his shoulders. He had proved himself as a writer and performer, and he confided to David Robinson of *The Sunday Times* about the project: 'I felt nervous about it, but I wanted to feel nervous . . . that's what I call "the good scared", where you bite off more than you can chew, and learn to chew bigger!' Responsibility for the film's $6 million budget was Simon's, since Warner Bros reasoned that the film's real chance of success lay with him, but when he delivered the finished film they were unsure what to do with it. Maybe they were expecting a 'sex and drugs and rock and roll' movie, or a tasteful vehicle which would appeal to the Simon fans who had bought *Bridge* in such quantities. What they got was a pensive, revealing film about an ageing rock star coming to terms with his life and the loss of his dreams. *Grease* it wasn't!

On its release, the film received only limited distribution in the States and remains unavailable on video. The film was screened in Holland soon after its US release, but it only received its British première in 1987 and disappeared immediately afterwards. It is a shame that *One Trick Pony* has not been more widely shown, for while it is flawed, it is one of the few films which successfully combines rock and roll with inherently believable characters and cohesive plot development. It also gave an airing to Simon's creative abilities away from the song format; his screenplay displayed a keen ear for dialogue and an unwillingness to rely on clichés.

Simon had specific aspirations for the film, and while not autobiographical there were still certain elements of Paul Simon in the character of Jonah Levin. 'People ask you, "Isn't it about time to stop playing rock and roll?"' Simon said at the time, 'yet nobody ever tells Stanley Kubrick, "You're fifty-one, now isn't it time to stop?" . . . I wanted to make a statement about the record industry which didn't fit into a three-minute pop song. The industry has been taken over by accountants and lawyers, which is a shame. You need people in it who like music.'

The music biz characters in *One Trick Pony* are largely un-sympathetic, with only Jonah's band displaying any redeeming features. It is a wry, compassionate film about a rock star pushing forty with a broken marriage behind him who faces the realization that he can never attain his dream of being a success on his own terms. The Jonah character, like his biblical namesake, never seems to get the breaks, and carries his bad luck with him like his guitar case. It's an epitaph for a generation who succumbed to rock and roll and watched it let them down, but who refuse to hang up their rock and roll shoes. On 'Jonah' Simon wistfully sings of '*all the boys who came along/carrying soft guitars in cardboard cases . . . do you wonder where those boys have gone?* Some went on to success, some went back to the real world, and some became like Jonah Levin, still fired by the ideal but realizing that his hour has long since passed.

As someone seemingly blessed with the Midas touch, *One Trick Pony* reveals a fallible side to Paul Simon. If 'The Sound of Silence' had been his only hit, Simon could well have found himself on one of those sad tour packages of 60s' Stars, who come on and play their hit to an ageing audience, determined not to admit that times have changed. It's a film for those with stardust memories, and indeed at one point in the film Jonah himself submits to a 'Salute to the Sixties' night, singing his one-dimensional, anti-Vietnam song 'Soft Parachutes'. It was a tricky moment, Paul Simon having to write the sort of song he probably would have written if he hadn't moved on, and it works sadly, brilliantly well, with Jonah backstage alongside other stars of the era like the Lovin' Spoonful and Tiny Tim. As if to say, there but for the grace of God goes Paul Simon!

Interesting enough as an insider's considered view of the rock industry, it is a bonus that Simon's script crackles with a laconic east coast humour. Allen Goorwitz's character Cal epitomizes all that Simon sees as wrong in the rock industry. A conceited, boastful man who prides himself on 'twenty years of AM ears', he vainly sounds off about who the real successes of the era are to a subdued Jonah: 'In fact, I said to the guy at *Billboard*, I said, "I'm a funny kind of guy, but I'll stick my neck out and say that Presley and the Stones are the only acts that successfully combined music and spectacle. Maybe Springsteen." ' 'How about Albert Schweitzer?' asks Jonah. 'You know, Africa, the organ, disease. Albert Schweitzer, the King of music and spectacle.' Without missing a beat, Cal asks 'What label's he on?' In rock film terms, only the spoof documentary *This Is Spinal Tap* matched Simon's pithy script.

The strengths of *One Trick Pony* are undeniably Simon's literate and believable script; his own performance, which manages to combine the winsome vulnerability of Jonah with a determination that is entirely credible; and a background which is authentic. Jonah and his band know that they're out of time, as in the scene where they quit the stage of Ohio's Agora Ballroom to let the B-52s on; their looks of blank incomprehension at one of the groups to whom the rock and roll baton has been passed speak volumes. Jonah, part of the first generation of rock and roll, now feels the generation gap bite. He still fervently admires the heroes of the 50s and 60s, but a new seething mob is rising for whom has-beens like Jonah have no relevance.

One Trick Pony is a sober reflection on those changing times and idols; the double irony which lays the film open to autobiographical interpretation is that it has Paul Simon playing a character whom Paul Simon could have been. Hovering ethereally over the film is the spirit of Elvis Presley, Simon's first hero. The man who lit the rock and roll fuse died in 1977, the year that Punk was at its screeching, snarling zenith.

While tiny Paul Simon from New York had realized long before that he could never be Elvis Presley, *One Trick Pony* is his statement that at least he tried. Simon had seen Elvis perform at Madison Square Garden in June 1972, which was astonishingly Elvis' New York debut. Simon was reticent about his opinion of the King's interpretation of his best-known song: 'I felt wonderful when he sang "Bridge Over Troubled Water", even though it was a touch on the dramatic side, but so was the song.'

The death of Elvis left a gaping hole; ironically the week he died was the week that Britain's *New Musical Express* carried the first advert for Elvis Costello's debut single. It marked a period of change, and for those who had followed in Elvis' wake it was a gap which could never be filled. Early on in *One Trick Pony*, Jonah's wife laceratingly confronts her husband. 'You have wanted to be Elvis Presley since you were thirteen years old. Well it's not a goal you're likely to achieve. He didn't do too well with it himself.' Later on, as Jonah and his band are whiling away the miles on their tour bus, they pass the time by playing 'rock and roll deaths'. As the depressing litany reels on – Hendrix, Morrison, Joplin, Eddie Cochran, Buddy Holly – Elvis' name is inevitably mentioned. 'Yeah,' Jonah sighs wistfully, 'he's dead.' Jonah's reconciliation with his wife comes with his intoning of Elvis' monologue from 'Are You Lonesome Tonight'.

From the film's opening montage, played out to the accompaniment of 'Late In The Evening', through to Simon's confrontation with a slickly unsympathetic record producer played by Lou Reed, *One Trick Pony* succeeds as a revelatory and credible music biz exposé. The *Los Angeles Times* called it 'an exceptionally handsome movie . . . an intimate film of much wit, style and impact. It ranks as one of the year's best.' In his entertaining 1987 book *Guide For The Film Fanatic*, Danny Peary listed *One Trick Pony* in his 'must see' category, one of an elite group of films which he claimed were 'essential viewing for the true film lover'; but they were in a minority. The reviews weren't so much hostile as non-existent. In the light of such subsequent self-indulgent efforts as Paul McCartney's *Give My Regards To Broad Street* and Prince's *Under A Cherry Moon*, *One Trick Pony* deserves a re-evaluation. There is much to enjoy and appreciate, and the film offers a promising indication of Simon's creative powers beyond 'the three-minute pop song'.

One of the advantages of the film from Warner's point of view was the soundtrack album, which was to be Simon's debut for the label; but after five years away from recording, the album was not a great success. It was too tied in with the film, which had sunk almost without trace. 'Late In The Evening' was a strong taster, and gave Simon a minor American hit; coming from a studio jam around Elvis' 'Mystery Train', the song rolls along, propelled by some thunderous Steve Gadd drumming and some vintage Simon scene setting: '*I'm with my troops, and down along the avenue, some guys were shootin' pool/And I heard the sound of acapella groups . . . singing late in the evening/And all the girls out on the stoops*'.

The title track contains a memorably compact Simon line about Jonah's plight, his performing urge being '*the principal source of his revenue*'. 'That's Why God Made The Movies' draws its imagery from François Truffaut's haunting film, *L'Enfant Sauvage*. 'Jonah' and 'God Bless The Absentee' are touchingly autobiographical songs about life on the road. The album's best song, though, is the poignant 'How The Heart Approaches What It Yearns', with the vivid opening lines: '*In the blue light of the Belvedere Motel/Wondering as the television burns/How the heart approaches what it yearns*'. It was a song Simon himself was particularly pleased with; pointing out its unorthodox time signature he said: 'I don't expect other people to notice it. But at least *I* know it.'

To promote the album, and to revitalize himself after the disappointment of *One Trick Pony*'s reception, Simon took to the road with his band from the film. A video of the 1980 tour shows how stilted Simon now sounded with the old Simon and Garfunkel material, only really coming alive with his solo work, specifically with the songs from the film. 'American Tune' is beautifully handled, its epic theme ringing down the years, still striking a response in an audience who were familiar with Simon's more introspective solo work. Returning for a solo 'The Sound of Silence', Simon again satisfied his audience with his recurring hymn of alienation. One incongruous note on the *One Trick Pony* tour was struck when Simon improbably segued 'Amazing Grace' into the Everlys' 'Bye Bye Love'.

Simon had a lot of catching up to do after his five-year absence, and made himself widely available for interviews in Europe. The most embarrassing of these was undoubtedly his encounter with Anne Nightingale on the BBC's venerable rock show *Whistle Test*. Ms Nightingale asked Simon how he was coping with writing songs without Art Garfunkel to help. Pointing out what the world already knew, Simon stated: 'We never wrote any songs together. I wrote all the songs. Not wishing to sound immodest, but Art only *sang* them with me.' The persistent Ms Nightingale asked if this was widely known. Simon replied: "I guess everyone knew except you."

At the Hammersmith Odeon, Simon delivered a spellbinding show, drawing on every facet of his career, delighting fervent fans with newly arranged versions of songs which were part of the popular vernacular, but which he could not leave alone and would constantly re-invent to satisfy himself. The tedium of running through a tried and tested set was not for him; while other artists may seek sanctuary in the familiarity of the past, Simon would always bend and twist the songs to see how much they could bear under the strain, and drag them into the present. The conclusion of the 1980 European tour was at Hammersmith, and Simon made a heartfelt speech from the stage, thanking the audience and wishing there was more he could do for them rather than just stand there and play his songs. Someone from the back of the circle called out, 'Buy us a drink then!', which Simon duly did, putting some money behind the bar of the Odeon to buy the 3,000 strong crowd a drink on him!

Interviewed by *Melody Maker* editor Ray Coleman in London in 1980, Simon was refreshingly candid about himself and his reputation. Bearing in mind his five-year hiatus from recording, he told Coleman: 'I assume no fans. That's quite truthful. I'm always a little scared when I put something out – I fear the people may have forgotten who I am. After all, there's such a lot of good music around, and it's very competitive. The public has a right not to like what I play. I never know whether the pulse of youth is running under my finger or whether I have my finger running *underneath* that pulse. I just put a finger out there and hope it's right.' But wherever he went, that public was always keen to know whether they'd ever see a Simon and Garfunkel reunion. Garfunkel had in fact joined Simon on stage in Paris during the 1980 tour, and the two had been in touch during the years since their split. Garfunkel's acting career had been in limbo since *Carnal Knowledge*; his first film since then – *Bad Timing* in 1979 – had been poorly received; united by the lack of success of their recent film efforts, and with a warming in the personal relationship between them, Simon and Garfunkel drifted back together at the beginning of the new decade.

Old Friends?

Paul Simon had been approached to play a free late summer concert in New York's Central Park in 1981. John Lennon's murder in December 1980 had robbed the music world of the one reunion which might really have rekindled the spirit of the 60s. The Stones were out playing to whole new audiences who came to gaze at the legends. There was a feeling of consolidating, of appraising the 60s and its icons with affection, a curiosity to see how they were weathering the test of time. Simon confessed that around the time he was 'still feeling a little shaky' after *One Trick Pony* and was in the middle of a periodic separation from Carrie. He considered asking Art Garfunkel to join him on stage in Central Park, initially for a short set, but then Simon realized he'd be in the invidious position of finding himself as an opening act for Simon and Garfunkel, and instead the two agreed to play the whole show together.

Preliminary meetings suggested the show could be a success and the creative partnership renewed. Both men were edging up to forty, and recently their solo careers had seemed to stagnate. The possibilities – both creative and financial – were considered. The timing seemed right, there was the beginning of a nostalgia boom for the 60s, and who could better epitomize those distant days than Simon and Garfunkel? 'We reminded ourselves of the humour we shared, the jokes, the similar concerns – the similarity of our lives,' recalled Garfunkel. There was an initial period of optimism that the old magic could be rekindled for just one night; Simon was swift to dismiss rumours that it was a purely financial concern: 'I don't think we'd get together if the potential for a joyous reunion weren't there. We'd never decide to grit our teeth just to make a couple of million dollars.'

Once in rehearsal, however, the old rivalries and friction swiftly surfaced. Garfunkel was insistent that a Simon and Garfunkel reunion should be a return to the spirit of their halcyon days, just

111

their two voices and one guitar; Simon, though, had never fully recovered from a hand injury of some years before, and playing solo guitar for anything up to three hours would be too onerous. He was also quick to point out that the bulk of his post-Simon and Garfunkel work was written with a large band specifically in mind – 'Kodachrome', 'Slip Slidin' Away' and 'Late In The Evening' just wouldn't sound right with only his guitar. Garfunkel eventually agreed and a full band was employed, although Simon later recalled the rehearsals for the Central Park reunion as 'miserable . . . Artie and I fought *all* the time'. Even around the time of the much publicized reunion, Garfunkel was telling a journalist about his relationship with Simon: 'This is a friendship to hold on to, but that also means it's someone who knows how to get under your skin, what buttons to push to make you a little crazy'; this hardly boded well for the keenly anticipated official reunion of the two 60s' icons.

A date was set for 19th September, 1981, and a large crowd was expected. Simon and Garfunkel were New York boys and many of their contemporaries felt the need to gather together to assuage the grief of Lennon's murder. Half a million people flocked to Central Park one chill autumn evening to see if a little bit of their collective past couldn't be snatched back for a night – to see if the preceding eleven years couldn't be held in abeyance for a few short hours, to try to pretend that Watergate and Cambodia hadn't happened, that the rise of Reagan to the White House could have been resisted and that '*Joltin' Joe*' hadn't gone away!

Once on stage, the old acrimonies and frictions disappeared in the welter of good feeling when New York's mayor, Ed Koch, took to the stage and simply announced, 'Ladies and gentlemen – Simon and Garfunkel'. 'It's great to do a neighbourhood concert,' cracked Simon near the beginning of the show, and the city responded with a roar that could be heard clear across the Brooklyn Bridge.

The Central Park show was an opportunity for the past to be relived for one incandescent night. All the familiar Simon and Garfunkel songs were delivered, and the audience had an opportunity to hear those comforting harmonies swirl together around more recent Simon songs like 'American Tune' (which Simon said he had always envisaged as a Simon and Garfunkel song) and 'Slip Slidin' Away'. The double album of the event reveals a muzak side to Simon and Garfunkel; the opening 'Mrs Robinson' is ragged, if right, but the handling of Simon and Garfunkel classics on this record leaves a lot to be desired – although as a souvenir of the event it's fine. There's an imaginative segue from 'Kodachrome' into Chuck Berry's automotive poem 'Maybellene', but the duo's handling of the Everly Brothers' perennial 'Wake Up Little Susie' is plain embarrassing – two forty-year-old men singing a song about being late home from a date!

The one new Simon original was the haunting 'Late Great Johnny Ace', a rock and roll triptych which begins life as a tribute to the young R&B singer who enjoyed such success with the poignant 'Pledging My Love', but died backstage on Christmas Eve 1954 while playing Russian roulette. Simon's lament infuses Ace's death with immense sadness and recalls the devotion inspired by singers in the first era of rock and roll; it then moves on to Simon's years in England, with the country reeling from the body blows of the Beatles and the Rolling Stones before culminating in a wistful reflection on the passing of John Lennon, and bringing the song full circle with a shared memory of the late, great Johnny Ace. The song took on an added poignancy when premièred in Central Park, just a motion away from the Dakota Building, site of Lennon's murder. Amidst all the public effusion at the Simon and Garfunkel reunion, the concert's most chilling moment occurred when a young man managed to burst on stage during Simon's performance of the song – to embrace? To assassinate? No one knew, and his only comment to the singer was 'I need to talk to you.' Simon was visibly shocked. In the atmosphere after Lennon's murder that anonymous man could so easily have been another Mark Chapman determined to make his mark on rock history.

For all the friction during rehearsals, once Simon and Garfunkel hit the stage and felt the waves of joy at their being together, the old magic was rekindled and both men believed that the buzz could well carry over onto a new studio album – their first since *Bridge Over Troubled Water* – and a world tour. Having just lost Simon to Warner Bros, CBS weren't slow off the mark in gaining some mileage out of their reunion, and ensured that *The Simon and Garfunkel Collection* was in the shops in time for Christmas 1981. The definitive seventeen-track compilation was a runaway success; in Europe alone it sold over two million copies, but such was the hurry to see it in the shops that the two men pictured on the moody cover aren't even Simon and Garfunkel, just a couple of look-alikes photographed somewhere on the Welsh coast!

Simon had already begun recording a new album, but the momentum of the Central Park show was such that he and Garfunkel felt sure it could be carried on for further shows. Perhaps it was all too rushed, perhaps the old magic had only actually lasted for the duration of the Central Park concert; whatever the reasons, the resultant world tour was an unhappy experience for both men. Simon later remembered it as 'unpleasant', with Garfunkel seeming 'always unhappy, everything was always tense'. Once on the road, the fissures between the two grew wider: 'We were hardly speaking' said Simon of that period during 1982/3 when the Simon and Garfunkel caravan rolled across the world, playing extensively in America, Europe and the Far East. Backstage it may well have been tense, with emissaries for the two stars liaising between camps; but once on stage their audiences continued to revel in the old chemistry. Playing giant stadiums, the unique intimacy and charm of a Simon and Garfunkel concert was lost; but for audiences that was hardly the point. Even from half a mile away, people were paying to be part of a lost childhood, to try to recapture some of the magic of their own adolescence in the company of two men who had played such a formative part in it. 'We were playing to 50,000 people a night,' recalled Simon three years later, 'they're paying us quarter of a million dollars a night, you sing 'Bridge Over Troubled Water', and everyone lights a candle – how did I screw you? Tell me again!' Candles were certainly lit, memories were shared, songs were sung, and the caravan rolled on to another stadium in another town, where another set of memories could be reawoken.

The real schism between Simon and Garfunkel came over the recording of their new album, widely heralded as the first together since *Bridge*; Simon found himself in the invidious position of having to top that classic for the second time, albeit twelve years on. The sessions for the album – which had the working title of *Think Too Much* – were tense and acrimonious. Simon was insistent that Garfunkel's vocal parts be completed prior to the tour; Garfunkel procrastinated, refusing to give up smoking and preferring to learn his parts by playing them on his Walkman during a walking tour of Switzerland. Simon bridled that the songs were among his most personal, largely dealing with his fractious relationship with Carrie, but was appeased when Garfunkel fairly pointed out that he understood the emotions the writer was dealing with. 'I understand what it is to be in love, to be in pain, to feel joy,' he told Simon, 'I'm a singer, I'm able to interpret. That's what I do!' In the event, Simon publicly denied that the new album was to be a Simon and Garfunkel collaboration and later denied rumours that he had wiped off Garfunkel's vocal tracks, saying none had ever been put

114

down. Simon went on to put the finishing touches to *his* new album: *Hearts & Bones*.

'People like the idea of reunions and happy endings,' Simon told David O'Donoghue. 'I never thought it would happen again, and I was reluctant to try. Not reluctant to try and do a concert – that's not impossible.' But of the recording, Simon described the sessions as a 'disaster', thereby laying the ghost of Simon and Garfunkel fully and finally. The two men had become victims of their own myth and the idea of a fully integrated reunion proved to be an impossibility, with the resultant arguments and eyeball-to-eyeball confrontations driving a wedge between them which time has barely tempered; the two of them only spoke again – for the first time in five years – at Garfunkel's father's funeral in 1986.

During the period after *One Trick Pony*, Simon later admitted that for the first time in his career he had been suffering 'a period of great depression . . . I was immobilised', and was in the depths of a writer's block from which he showed no signs of emerging. It took a Los Angeles psychiatrist called Rod Gorney to help Simon conquer his feelings of inadequacy. In his long, revelatory *Playboy* interview in 1984 he said: 'He was able to penetrate someone whose defences were seemingly impenetrable. He was able to make me feel that I wasn't there to work just for the satisfaction of having a hit but that there was a contribution to be made. Of course, the reason I'd been blocked was that I felt what I did was of absolutely no importance. He was able to say "I'm telling you that the way to contribute is through your songs. And it's not for you to judge their merits, it's for you to write the songs". For me that was brilliant – and liberating.'

Despite being Simon's lowest-selling album in twenty years, *Hearts and Bones* is by no means an artistic failure, and it is certainly his most intense work to date. Simon had always managed to distance himself from his work; even *Still Crazy After All These Years* had retained a degree of objectivity. As a writer, Simon assimilated, sifted and distilled experiences but ultimately distanced himself from them in his songs. On *Hearts and Bones* though, Simon was committing himself both artistically and emotionally. Having conquered his writer's block, Simon had spent the summers of 1981 and 1982 carefully fashioning songs, only one of which failed to appear on the finished album – the strongly anti-nuclear 'Citizen of the Planet', which Simon considered 'too direct'.

The opening track of 1983's *Hearts and Bones*, 'Allergies', refers directly to Simon's preoccupation with his hand injury: '*My hand*

115

can't touch a guitar string/My fingers just burn and ache'; while 'The Late Great Johnny Ace' was a rare diary entry from a writer who usually kept his innermost thoughts to himself. 'René and Georgette Magritte With Their Dog After the War' was the title of a photo caption which Simon immediately felt was 'an interesting title for a song', while realizing, as he told *Rolling Stone*'s David Fricke, that it was not 'in any form or incarnation going to be a popular record'. The song was an appropriately surreal tableau about the Belgian artist which also featured a litany of doo-wop groups – the Penguins, the Moonglows, the Orioles, the Five Satins – culled from Simon's memory of New York radio shows in the 1950s.

'Song About The Moon' again seems autobiographical, Simon the tunesmith – who had just emerged from a writer's block – addressing his audience about songwriting: *'If you want to write a song about the moon/You want to write a spiritual tune/Then do it!'* Simon had actually been listening to Sam Cooke's 'Bring It On Home' and played around with the chord structure to arrive at his finished song. 'Cars Are Cars' was based on the memory of Simon's first set of wheels, the short-lived 1958 Impala – the fruits of his early success with 'Hey Schoolgirl' – and ends with the wry observation, *'If some of my homes had been more like my car/I probably wouldn't have travelled this far'* which could well stand as Bruce Springsteen's epitaph!

The album's title track was even more vividly autobiographical, an account of Simon's stormy relationship with Carrie Fisher, the couple *'returning to their natural coasts . . . speculate who had been damaged the most'*. The *'one and one-half wandering Jews'* in the song's opening line refer to Simon himself and Carrie, whose father Eddie Fisher was Jewish. Both versions of 'Think Too Much' also dwell on his relationship with Carrie, carried on under the bright glare of press interest in the couple. Simon's recent bout of analysis had given him a more heightened sense of self-awareness and in these two tracks he recognizes one of his own faults with the line *'maybe I think too much for my own good'*.

'Train In The Distance' is quite explicitly about Simon's first marriage. The opening line refers to his ex-wife Peggy, who was already married when they met, *'as beautiful as Southern skies'*. Simon pans out from the specific relationship to a wider perspective with the chorus. He told *Playboy*: 'I happened to use the train metaphor because I was sitting in a friend's house, near a railway station, and I heard a train . . . there's something about the sound of a train that's very romantic and nostalgic and hopeful.'

116

'The Late Great Johnny Ace' stands as the album's masterpiece and continues the themes Simon considered so maturely in *One Trick Pony*. Using the late R&B singer as his starting point and conclusion, Simon parallels his own life and also evokes the late, great John Lennon without resorting to the pomposity or hollow reverence other writers have fallen into. The song's haunting coda was orchestrated by Philip Glass, for whose fascinating 1986 album *Songs From Liquid Days* Simon contributed the lyrics to 'Changing Opinion', an enigmatic piece which draws on the tonality of sheer noise, acting as a Proustian trigger to the past: *'Maybe it's the hum of a calm refrigerator cooling on a big night/Maybe it's the hum of our parents' voices long ago in a soft light'*. Glass had approached songwriters of stature, including Simon, David Byrne, Suzanne Vega and Laurie Anderson, because they were 'not only outstanding songwriters on their own but also lyricists whose poetry reflects individual styles and approaches to songwriting'.

The sense of rock and roll tradition characterized by 'Johnny Ace' was something that Simon was particularly aware of during the recording of *Hearts and Bones*, with 'Bring It On Home' as a starting point for 'Song About The Moon'. Simon told Andy Peebles (ironically, the last journalist to interview John Lennon): 'There was a break in recording, and we couldn't think what to do, so we got a pile of old records, and one of the first we played was an old 45 of 'Earth Angel' by the Penguins; and it was a terrible, scratched, warped old single coming out from these great big speakers in the control room, and it had a tremendous effect on me. Here was a record I had been hearing for twenty-seven years; every year, somewhere, you'd hear "Earth Angel", and listening to it then there was such a tremendous sense of our own mortality.' That sense of the importance of pop music reinforces something which fellow traveller Bruce Springsteen was aware of when he told Dave Marsh in 1980: 'There's this song, "Jungle Rock" by Hank Mizell . . . what a mysterious person. What a ghost. And you can put that thing on and see him . . . standing in some little studio, way back when, and just singing that song. No reason, nothing gonna come of it. Didn't sell. That wasn't no Number 1 record, and he wasn't playing no big arenas either. . . . But what a mythic moment, what a mystery. Those records are filled with mystery. . . . The joy and abandon, inspiration. Inspirational records!'

Despite quintessential Simon songs such as the title track, 'Train in the Distance', and 'Johnny Ace', *Hearts and Bones* beached on its release. It was a dispiriting experience for Simon to find that his

117

audience had moved on. The break-up of his marriage to Carrie Fisher exacerbated the situation, and while his former glories ensured a comfortable income well into his dotage, Paul Simon found himself in a creative cul-de-sac. He genuinely felt that songs like 'René and Georgette Magritte . . .' and 'Johnny Ace' were experimental and deserved a wider audience; in a revealing interview with Vin Scelsa in 1986, Simon looked back on the album: 'I was unprepared for something that wasn't a hit. Playing it again, it doesn't even sound like a hit to me! . . . It appeared that what I was interested in was not what the vast majority of people are interested in. Certainly, it is not what radio is playing. . . . So I said to myself, "Well, really the last thing I feel like doing is sitting down with my guitar and writing another song that I think is interesting that nobody's gonna play. . . ." Careers do have an arc to them, and one's popularity doesn't necessarily have to follow the popularity level of your work. It is possible that to become less popular and to actually continue to do good work, or even better work than your most popular work and if that is the case, that's my job to keep doing as good work as I can. I do hope it's popular because it really means that people have heard it, if people hear it and reject it that's cool, if people don't hear it, it's frustrating.'

That frustration did erode Simon's hard-won confidence. He was used to sales stretching into seven figures but the returns on *Hearts and Bones* were a small fraction of that. At forty-two, Paul Simon seemed to have little in common to offer an audience growing interested in the rootsier rock and roll of new bands like Jason and the Scorchers, REM, the Beat Farmers, True West and Los Lobos, bands characterized by a kick-ass attitude to rock, determined to plant some post-Punk roots.

Paul Simon's stature was such that decreased sales and output did little to affect his reputation within the music business, and he was among the phalanx of superstars drafted in on 28th January, 1985 to sing on USA For Africa's 'We Are The World'. Simon flew in from New York especially for the session, which found him standing next to a blank space marked 'Prince', which was never filled. 'Check Your Egos at the Door' begged Quincy Jones' sign at the studio entrance. It was a truly staggering panorama of talent which gathered that night, the first time that Dylan and Simon had appeared on record together. The LA glitz of the occasion, however, left those who had witnessed the endearingly shaggy spontaneity of Band Aid's 'Do They Know It's Christmas?' a few months before, aghast. The USA For Africa tee-shirts were already printed up, and the appalling irony of the lavish banquet laid on after the session seemed to escape those in attendance. It took Bob Geldof to remind the participants that 'the price of a life this year is a piece of plastic seven inches across'.

Simon spoke movingly about his involvement in USA For Africa: 'When something like this comes along that allows everyone to participate and feel you're making a contribution, you rush to do it, because otherwise you feel you're just a witness to a tragedy.' Simon was set to duet with Dylan ('I can sing harmony with most people') at Live Aid that June, but like a number of surprises that day, the duet failed to materialize.

It was a time in his life when Simon felt the future was slip slidin' away. One thing seemed certain, though, even to his most devoted fans: whatever convulsive force would next affect the future of rock and roll, Paul Simon would have no part in it. Until one day in the summer of 1984 when a guitarist friend of Simon's called Heidi Berg innocently passed him an unlabelled bootleg tape of music from the black townships of South Africa.

Under African Skies

Ironically it was a bootleg cassette which led to Paul Simon embarking on the *Graceland* project. While the sleeve of his finished album may state 'Unauthorized duplication is a violation of applicable laws', Simon was blithely unconcerned about how the tape *Gumboots: Accordion Jive Hits, Vol. II* had arrived with him that summer of 1984; what fascinated him, and led to his total commitment over the ensuing three years, was the music which it contained: Mbaqanga, or 'township jive'.

The tape couldn't have arrived in Simon's life at a more fortuitous time. Artistically, he had been drifting too far from the shore, and his second marriage was on the rocks. Despite global success with Simon and Garfunkel, a distinguished twelve-year solo career and sporadic diversions into film and television, Simon was at a creative nadir. By the mid-80s, Simon was concentrating most of his energies on rearing his only son Harper, and the *Gumboots* tape arrived at a propitious moment. 'Otherwise I wasn't doing anything,' he admitted, sounding like a latterday Jay Gatsby, 'I was just sitting looking out at the sea.'

That Paul Simon had no need ever to lift a guitar again was not in doubt. While too rarely bracketed alongside rock poets like Dylan or Lennon, Simon's painstaking approach to rock music had seen him firmly entrenched as one of the genre's most admired and successful composers. Money was never the motivating factor for Simon; artistic impetus was paramount. 'I'm not really all that interested in the hits. I'm more concerned with losing touch to a really significant degree with my generation,' Simon told David Hepworth in 1986, 'they don't listen to music as much as they did, or if they do, they listen to the old music. So the chance to talk about what life is like for us, as we pass through the different stages, is not something that rock'n'roll has been the medium for. . . . I believe in the power of rock'n'roll to affect people and I'd like to see it able to handle more mature subject matter. We all grew up with rock'n'roll, and for us it's never going to go away.'

That is the connection which fired Simon: in *Gumboots* he felt again the excitement and musical freshness which first made him want to pick up a guitar as a solitary teenager in New York City in the early 50s. On that tape he heard echoes of the Moonglows, the Orioles, the Monotones, the Bobettes, the Satins . . . but criss-crossed with extraordinary rhythms and metres which fell beyond even Simon's conscientiously expanded frames of reference. It was all there, on that vital tape – both creatively and personally, *Gumboots* offered Simon a challenge.

Throughout his professional career, Simon had demonstrated an extraordinary facility for assimilating diverse influences into his own music without making them bland or ostentatiously novel. On his records since 1972, elements such as reggae, South American folk, rhythm & blues, calypso, Gospel, Latin American and jazz had been successfully integrated. Mbaqanga, however, presented technical problems on a musical level which Simon had never encountered before. His knowledge of African music prior to that summer had been limited to that of Miriam Makeba, her former husband trumpeter Hugh Masekela, Fela Kuti, King Sunny Ade and Ladysmith Black Mambazo whom he knew from the 1978 BBC documentary *Rhythm of Resistance: The Music of South Africa.*

Throughout the summer of 1984 Simon immersed himself in the indigenous black music of South Africa, picking his way through twenty or so albums which represented the very best of that rich culture. 'Over the summer, I tried to absorb the musical essence of the music, which was difficult, because the shape of the songs were not what I was used to.' Eventually the nagging rhythms and fractured structures wormed their way into Simon's musical subconscious and he began scat singing over the songs, applying melodies and fragmentary lyrics to existing songs.

With no other diversions, and fired by the vitality of the music, Simon decided to take the project one step further, and this is where the real controversy over *Graceland* arose. Simon, accompanied by his long-time friend and colleague Roy Halee, flew to Johannesburg to try and contact the musicians who had played on the *Gumboots* tape with an eye to recording with them for some as yet embryonic project.

Prior to Simon and Halee's visit to South Africa, the musicians with whom Simon was keen to work took a vote on whether his presence there would be a good thing: 'They decided that my coming would benefit them because I could help to give South African music a place in the international community of music similar to that of reggae.' In New York, before the trip, Simon also consulted Quincy Jones and Harry Belafonte, both of whom have close links with the South African musical community. They both backed him in his decision.

In retrospect Simon has been loudly criticized for tracing the music back to its source: why did he have to *go* there? His stay, critics argued, aided and abetted the South African economy. Why couldn't he work with exiled South African musicians? Why couldn't he record in Zimbabwe? But from the outset, Simon perceived the South African sessions as an integral part of his cultural odyssey: 'At first I thought, "It's too bad this isn't from Zimbabwe or Zaire or Nigeria, because life would be simpler". But then I thought, "It's beautiful, I like it, I want to see if I can inter-act with it musically". . . . I'm not a musicologist, I didn't go to make an archival album of South African music, but an album of *my* music with musicians I could inter-act with. . . . I learned a long time ago that if you want to work in a different idiom, you can't simply imitate what you hear. Your ears aren't trained to the nuances. You've got to go to the source. So I went to Africa.'

The Johannesburg sessions took place over two and a half weeks in February 1985. Producer Hilton Rosenthal, who was a major force in the development of South African music, had put Simon in touch with the groups who had appeared on the *Gumboots* tape, including General M. D. Shirinda and The Gaza Sisters, Tao Ea Matsekha (the Lion of Matsekha) and the Boyoyo Boys. The core musicians in South Africa were guitarist Ray Phiri and drummer Isaac Mtshali from the group Stimela, and Matsekha's bassist, Baghiti Khumalo. As if to assure the musicians of his integrity, Simon paid them triple American Musicians Union rates and took pains to ensure that they would also receive performers' royalties.

In the first week of recording at Johannesburg's Ovation Studios, Simon cut a song appropriately called 'Gumboots' and 'The Boy In The Bubble'; during the next ten days, 'Graceland', 'I Know What I Know' and 'Crazy Love Vol. II' were laid down. Simon had no songs prepared prior to his trip, and the lyrics and melodies were improvised in the studio over the basic rhythms from the *Gumboots* tape. Many of the South African musicians were oblivious to Simon's stature, but there was an immediate empathy in the studio, a spontaneous musical communion which Simon eagerly responded to: 'They were very rewarding and very demanding sessions. I was following impulses, making up the songs around the basic music I was getting, shaping as I went along. At the same time I was working through translators, trying to describe the music through talking about chords and notes. With some of the traditional artists . . . that was impossible. That wasn't how they understood making music.'

Simon was so inspired by the music which had propelled him to South Africa, and so fired by what was being created in tandem in the studio, that he felt impelled to share writing credits on the finished album. Five of the album's finished songs bear co-writing credits – an indication of the huge debt Simon felt he owed to the South African musicians. Only the contentious 'Scarborough Fair' had featured Garfunkel as co-author, while 1970's 'El Condor Pasa' had Simon's English lyrics grafted onto a traditional Peruvian melody arranged by Jorge Milchberg and Daniel Robels. *Paul Simon* in 1972 featured the fascinating co-writing credit 'Simon & Grappelli' on 'Hobo's Blues' and his spell in London in the mid-60s had seen a number of Simon-Woodley compositions. Sharing the writing credits for some of the *Graceland* songs was a vital way of ensuring that the money from royalties would reach the people who had directly helped Simon in his realization of the album.

How scrupulous Simon was, though, in acknowledging his American collaborators is open to question – the melody of 'That Was Your Mother' is certainly similar to Rockin' Dopsie's own 'My Baby She's Gone' from his 1979 album *Hold On*. Los Lobos' Cesar Rosas had mixed feelings about the band's session for *Graceland*: 'We thought he was going to have some songs. I mean, Paul Simon, who's got songs coming out of his ears, right? But he didn't have any, he was waiting for us to write something, and we don't really work like that.' Rosas and his co-writer David Hidalgo told *Guitarist* magazine that they came up with the rough melody of 'All Around The World Or The Myth Of Fingerprints' but received no credit for it on the album; Hidalgo recalled the sessions: 'It was like, "go ahead, start playing", no direction at all!' At one stage in mid-1987, Los Lobos seriously considered suing Simon for what they saw as his hijacking of their melody, but later felt that the resultant publicity would prompt him into 'doing something about it'.

In his efforts to 'integrate South African music with his own musical impulses', the bulk of Simon's seventeen days in South Africa were spent in the recording studios; even so Simon couldn't help but be aware of being inside a country under siege. He told

Hot Press: 'You really can't miss it, the feeling of the whole society is terribly strained with racial tension. It's not like any other thing I've ever felt. Even coming from a country that's got its own history of racial antagonism and abuses, this was something beyond anything I've ever seen before.'

One Sunday Simon did take a break from recording and drove out to Soweto: 'It was nothing like I pictured it to be. I thought it would be like Bedford Stuyvesant, a New York ghetto, but it's twenty square miles and with two million people. On the surface there was an appearance of normality but a definite tension underneath . . . as you talk to people, you realize that you are in a country that is in the grip of a tremendous social upheaval; a nation that is grappling with a political problem that really no other nation in the world has to deal with, which is, can there be an effective transference of power in a peaceful way or will there be another war, similar to what happened in Zimbabwe?'

Throughout the controversy which was later to engulf *Graceland*, Paul Simon stressed that it was 'a musical odyssey' which had taken him to South Africa. The finished album certainly reaffirms Simon's musical quest, incorporating as it does Mbaqanga, cajun and rock and roll – unified by accordion and saxophone, and made cohesive by Simon's own intuitive musical genius.

The album is infused with an exhilaration, an exuberance which reflects Simon's delight at having successfully integrated his own music with that of other cultures. There is the choral discipline of Ladysmith Black Mambazo, the driving new-wave rock and roll of Los Lobos, the ebullience of Rockin' Dopsie, and overall Paul Simon as maestro of an orchestra bridging two continents.

'The Boy In The Bubble' and 'Graceland' are the striking opening salvo of the album, undeniably in the pop tradition but startlingly fresh and innovative, setting a pace which is miraculously maintained over the whole album. The bracing accordion and drum introduction of 'The Boy In The Bubble' leads into one of the decade's most perfectly realized songs. The '*days of miracle and wonder*' fly in the face of the pessimism of the 80s: with the biblical scale of AIDS, massive unemployment, the proliferation of nuclear weapons, the callous indifference of conservative governments in America and Britain and terrorism running riot, they may seem more like days of chaos and disharmony; but Simon delights in the creative, positive use of technology and the inherent possibility of mankind, offering hope and optimism to convince us that these truly are '*days of miracle and wonder*'. The song, particularly the first verse, was inspired by Simon's observations of events in South Africa, and along with the title track took the longest to write. The song's central images came from scientific magazines Simon had been reading which had struck him with their 'poetic language'. Ultimately, he told David Fricke, 'The Boy In The Bubble' devolved down to 'hope and dread . . . that's the way I see the world, a balance between the two, but coming down on the side of hope'. If anything, Simon had learned from his South African experience that hope for a bright, free future remains essential – in the face of repression optimism is the unchallenged pre-requisite.

Simon's brilliance on this album is in marrying quite disparate strands of music to his own inimitable vision, combining and enhancing a style of music alien to both himself and his audience. The most successful fusion occurs on the title track of *Graceland*. Throughout his career, from the Tom and Jerry days thirty years before, through Elvis' Vegas years and the reflections of *One Trick Pony*, Paul Simon was drawn by the magnetism of Elvis Presley. It is fitting therefore that the title of Simon's finest album should come from the mansion of his mentor – 'Graceland'. It is appropriate, too, that the harmony vocals were by Don and Phil Everly, the brothers who directly influenced the nascent Simon and Garfunkel.

Simon symbolizes Elvis' Memphis home as a musical Canaan, a promised land for each successive generation which succumbs to rock and roll, where, one day, '*we all will be received*'. From the striking opening image of the Mississippi Delta '*shining like a National Guitar*', through the idea of Graceland itself as a sanctuary for ghosts and pilgrims searching for salvation, the song is at once a tribute and a caution. Simon told Vin Scelsa: 'The reason that I called the album *Graceland* is that this theme comes up unintentionally in about five or six of the songs. I didn't name the album until after I'd finished writing all the songs, but I noticed that same kind of spiritual awakening, that search for tranquility or some kind of discovery of a greater idea than the self.' It was that quest which drew Paul Simon to South Africa.

On 'Under African Skies' Simon audaciously tells '*the story of how we begin to remember*', and signposts the album's main musical theme, '*These are the roots of rhythm/And the roots of rhythm remain*'. One of the themes of *Graceland* is the unifying power of music in a world rent asunder by political differences, and in 'Under African Skies' Paul Simon manages to effect a reconciliation between Linda Ronstadt growing up in Arizona and Joseph Shabalala's childhood in Africa. Ronstadt is also the guest vocalist on the track, an unfortunate and ironic choice as she was one of the few artists of the Woodstock generation who played Sun City – but Simon is determined to show that friendship and music transcend politics; a fact which Miriam Makeba proved when she made the song her own in concert.

For Paul Simon, the undoubted musical highlight of *Graceland* was the opportunity to work with Ladysmith Black Mambazo. The group – whose name literally translates as 'The Black Axe of Ladysmith' – sprang from the musical vision of their leader Joseph Shabalala. Joseph was born in 1942 in Ladysmith, a town in South Africa's Natal province. In the late 50s, he was forced to move to Durban to find work and it was there that he served his musical apprenticeship with the Highlanders, before forming a group with relatives in 1958 which became Ladysmith Black Mambazo in 1972. The acapella music and choreographed movements of Ladysmith spring from dormitory-dwelling black migrant workers; a constant supply of cheap labour is always needed in the towns, so the workers – removed from home and family – have perforce evolved their own cheap entertainment. Under the leadership of Joseph Shabalala, Ladysmith Black Mambazo have become one of South Africa's most successful indigenous acts; a fact which is all the more astonishing when you realize that Joseph can neither read nor write music – but he manages to convey his purpose and compose the rich harmonies of Ladysmith orally.

During rehearsals for the *Graceland* shows at the Royal Albert Hall in 1987, I was lucky enough to spend some time talking with Joseph Shabalala. He is without doubt one of the nicest artists it has ever been my pleasure to meet, exuding a serenity and dignity remarkable in one who has laboured his whole life under the yoke of apartheid. Ladysmith's success at home means that they work arduously – although in 1980 Joseph made the decision to cut down their concerts from four hours to a more manageable three! Joseph was already vaguely aware of Simon's music when he was approached to appear with Ladysmith on *Graceland*, having borrowed a tape of *Bridge Over Troubled Water* from a neighbour.

Shabalala and Simon worked together on 'Homeless', and so inspired was Simon by Joseph's musical input that he wrote 'Under African Skies' about the Ladysmith leader. Joseph is eulogistic when speaking of his mentor and was delighted when Simon produced Ladysmith's *Shaka Zulu* album in 1986 – an event which he called 'the most exciting adventure of our lives'. Simon and Roy

Halee, who engineered the album, were more painstaking in their production than Joseph had been used to when recording in South Africa: 'We rehearse at home, we do everything perfect there, then we tell the producer we're ready and go to the studio one day, for maybe eight or ten hours and we finish the whole ten or twelve songs. The next day it is for the producer to mix the record.' Not surprisingly, the Simon/Halee method took slightly longer!

'I like Paul Simon,' declared Joseph enthusiastically, 'you know why? He is a musician. I am sure he is not like other producers who don't know how to sing. You see, Paul Simon chooses what he likes and he tells you "this is good because of this and this", and he expects you to talk with him and tell him what is right and what is wrong. He is very nice to work with, he is a polite guy who likes to hear your suggestions.'

It was Joseph Shabalala who sat beside Paul Simon at the *Graceland* press conference and winningly described music as 'something you can't hinder, it goes from here straight up to Heaven'. He denied that Ladysmith Black Mambazo had any political 'message', but remained calm even while criticizing those who had attacked Paul Simon over his recording in South Africa: 'Those who criticize Paul Simon and say that he did wrong to come and do this thing, they themselves are now ashamed, because so many people have said this is good – especially my group. It was my chance, this was a good opportunity to disclose our music all over the world, because many people didn't know this kind of music. . . . I say that what Paul Simon did for us is good.'

It was a two-way relationship. Simon was unreservedly enthusiastic about the fluency and vivacity of Ladysmith's work, calling them 'the best harmony group in the world'. He did however have his doubts about being able to integrate with them musically and told Vin Scelsa: 'Joseph gave me a lot of Ladysmith albums, and after working in the studio in South Africa I'd go back and listen to them on my Walkman – fall asleep listening to Ladysmith Black Mambazo. I didn't think I'd really be able to work with them, their harmonies and their counterpoint seemed so intricate. . . . I was actually intimidated to suggest working together, but as the album took shape, and looked as though it was going to be about different types of South African music, I realized it would be great if I could get a track with Ladysmith.'

Simon had a fragment of a song floating around his head, *'moonlight sleeping on a midnight lake'*, which he demoed – multi-tracking himself to suggest the effect of Ladysmith Black Mambazo

– and mailed to Joseph. 'I sent a letter saying this is a sketch of a song, you can change the melodies or harmonies. . . . You can change the lyrics, or add lyrics in Zulu, make any changes you want.' Using London's legendary Abbey Road studios as a halfway house, Simon and Roy Halee recorded what was to become 'Homeless' with Ladysmith in October 1985. Joseph had contributed some Zulu lyrics to Simon's demo, and working with him, Simon wrote an English phrase to accompany Joseph's lyric. This was recorded in one day; overnight Joseph lifted a Zulu wedding melody and added some more words which fitted in with the theme of 'Homeless' and the next day it was finished.

For those who carped that *Graceland* had no political message, 'Homeless' deserves repeated listening. Both Hugh Masekela and Miriam Makeba spoke emphatically of the song as their own anthem, and the chorus '*Strong wind, destroy our home,/Many dead tonight, it could be you*' is a compelling symbol of the bloody apocalypse towards which South Africa is hurtling.

The collaboration continued with the jubilant 'Diamonds On The Soles Of Her Shoes', which was recorded in New York six months later. The song is perhaps the most striking fusion on the album – Ladysmith's Zulu overture slipping effortlessly into Simon's urbane, urban lyrics. The title alone is striking, drawing attention to the poor little rich girl, whose remedy for '*the walking blues*' is wearing diamonds on the soles of her shoes!

While it is undoubtedly the music and rhythms of oppressed black South Africa which dominate *Graceland*, the album acts as a cultural bridge over the troubled waters of politics; in a cultural cross-pollination quite unlike any other in rock's history, it also encompasses the bravura bayou swing of Rockin' Dopsie's cajun and the energetic Chicano rock and roll of Los Lobos. For Simon the instruments of unification were the saxophone and accordion. Rock music has always placed the saxophone in a position of unhealthy reverence – the E. Street Band's Clarence Clemons, Gerry Rafferty's 'Baker Street', Roxy Music's Andy McKay; but the accordion has remained largely under-used – one remembers fondly Johnnie Allen's swaggering version of Chuck Berry's 'The Promised Land', Joe Ely's Ponty Boone and Richard Thompson's use of accordionist John Kirkpatrick. It was saxophonist Richard Landry – who has worked with everyone from Otis Redding through to Laurie Anderson – who introduced Simon to Rockin' Dopsie in his native Louisiana, thereby forging another link in the chain.

As a musical style, cajun has rarely entered the pop music

mainstream, save for sporadic championing by Creedence Clear-water Revival and Ry Cooder; but Simon's choice of Rockin' Dopsie was astute – along with Clifton Chenier and Queen Ida, Dopsie was the leading exponent of the driving cajun/zydeco music which proliferates around the bayou of the deep South. 'That Was Your Mother' brilliantly captures a sweaty Saturday night on the bayou – juxtaposed is the pure image of the young girl *'pretty as a prayerbook, sweet as an apple on Christmas Day'*.

As well as exploring the music of a new continent, *Graceland* led Simon to rediscover the joys of indigenous American music. By the time of *Graceland*, Los Lobos had released two albums which saw them established as firm critics' favourites, but popular success did not come their way until 1987 when they had a Number 1 British and American single with the theme from the film *La Bamba*. Simon was familiar with the band's work, and their use of saxophone and accordion incorporated a theme which he was keen to use on his album.

The Los Lobos track 'All Around The World Or The Myth Of Fingerprints' uses the recurrent figure of the chat show host, who Simon saw as a sort of 'modern historian . . . the perspective on what life is like in our culture'. But running deeper than that, the lyrics reflect the state of things in South Africa. Simon used the metaphor of fingerprints to show that 'there's a lot more similarities that we have than differences. That seemed to me a statement that I could make comfortably at the end of this album that dealt with different cultures and different people, I wanted to say that we're *not* different. On a political level, in fact, if you want to think about people as being the same as you it's harder to kill them!'

Uncertain of just how *Graceland* would be received, his bedrock audience having evaporated by the time of *Hearts and Bones*, Simon dipped his toe in the water by releasing 'You Can Call Me Al' as the album's first single in the middle of 1986. The lyrics sprang from a misunderstanding between Paul, his then wife Peggy, and the composer Pierre Boulez, following a party at the Simons' apart-ment in the early 70s: on leaving, Boulez thanked his hosts, 'Al' and 'Betty'. The title is also one of the lines in the classic 30s' Depression song, 'Brother, Can You Spare A Dime?'

The staccato rhythms of 'You Can Call Me Al' were immediately appealing and unusual, and so was the accompanying video. Actor Chevy Chase was an old friend of Simon's from *Saturday Night Live*, and had guested in 1985 on Paul McCartney's video for 'Spies Like Us'. What made the 'You Can Call Me Al' video so outstanding in the days of big budget, dry ice spectaculars was its innate simplicity – no madly infuriating cross-cuts or frenetic editing; instead one camera stayed fixed on one shot of one set, while Chase confused first-time buyers by appearing to *be* Paul Simon, who appeared as a guest in his own video, a Buster Keaton figure doing his own roadying.

The success of the first single and *Graceland* the album was instantaneous – the album has remained in the British and American charts since its release in September 1986. A further three singles have been lifted off the album – 'The Boy In The Bubble', 'Graceland' and 'Under African Skies'. The video for 'The Boy In The Bubble' was outstanding. Simon utilized state of the art video technology with 3-D graphics which brilliantly illustrated the song's vivid imagery. Simon also filmed a video for 'Homeless', which incorporated news footage of 'disturbances' in South Africa. Needless to say it was banned by the broadcasting authorities there, a fact Simon's critics conveniently overlooked.

Pop in the 1980s wasn't short of gimmicks, but *Graceland* (and its accompanying videos) went far beyond the headline-catching gimmickry of contemporary pop. The immediate reaction against Punk in Britain in the early 80s was characterized by the New Romantic movement, stylish and androgynously elegant, personified by Boy George, whom Fleet Street effectively destroyed as instantly as they had created. The style of 80s pop was 'safe'. Wham!, Duran Duran, Spandau Ballet and Swing Out Sister represented a conservative face, superficial and escapist. Excellent new acts such as Eurythmics and Paul Young posed little threat to the established order, while manufactured scams like Sigue Sigue Sputnik and the Beastie Boys were best forgotten.

With an upwardly mobile generation hungry for CD sounds, unremarkable albums from Sade, Dire Straits and Phil Collins were in the ascendant; even the industry's established megastars like Elton John, Paul McCartney and David Bowie fell victim to dipping record sales. Bruce Springsteen's 1984 *Born In The USA* marked a return to traditional rock values, but the decade was dominated by Michael Jackson's 1983 *Thriller*, which shifted an incredible thirty-eight million copies. Record buyers were playing it safe, and the innately conservative record industry became stale and predictable, a situation practised music biz veteran Paul Simon recognized. He spoke to Vin Scelsa in September 1986, prior to the success of *Graceland*: 'Every time there's a significant increase in the amount of money being made, I think there's a corresponding decrease in the quality of the music. If you look at the 50s when rock and roll first started, all those first records came out of little independent companies; as soon as rock and roll got into the big companies in the late 50s and early 60s, the days of the teen idols from Philadelphia, selling becomes a very important aspect, and the music quality dips. It didn't pick up again until things from Liverpool broke out, and that was again a little provincial scene that infused the rest of the 60s. The folk scene again didn't have much to do with corporate profit. . . . I think every time people think in terms of packaging, of demographics, of giving people what they want, the music becomes more sterilized, more to do with style or fashion than it has to do with music, and the quality dips down.'

In the context of Paul Simon's career, *Graceland* is a creative rebirth, a renaissance which finds one of the 60s' finest songwriters drawing positive energy from a new and vibrant source. As if to prove that the music which inspired him had such a revelatory effect, Simon's singing on the album – notably on 'Crazy Love' and 'Under African Skies' – is amongst the best of his career. Lyrically the album is acutely, at times painfully, autobiographical; dealing with his divorce from Carrie Fisher, the intense joy of parenthood and his discovery of a vital new vein of music. Gone is the petulant isolationism of 'I Am A Rock' and 'The Dangling Conversation'. The pleasure of working with the joyous acapella community which is Ladysmith Black Mambazo provides a soulful counterpoint to Simon's own voice.

Graceland bubbles over with the warmth of a new-found musical fellowship: from the linguistic somersaults of 'You Can Call Me Al' and uplifting harmonies of 'Homeless' to the rock and roll pilgrimage of 'Graceland' and the exuberant 'Diamonds On The Soles Of Her Shoes'. From the spiritual 'Under African Skies' and the jagged accordion of Forere Motloheloa ushering in 'The Boy In The Bubble', through Baghiti Khumalo's soaring bass run climaxing 'Al' and the intense fractured rhythms of Stimela, to Simon's buoyant rise through the register at the end of 'Crazy Love', the album's theme is that of an odyssey. Simon, a stranger in the Third World, *'surrounded by the sound'* and searching out the *'roots of rhythm'*. Simon reflected on the album to Gene Santoro of *Pulse*: 'I noticed after I'd finished writing all the songs that a lot of them had a very similar theme: acceptance, aiming at some state of peace, looking for some state of redemption or grace. That was the theme of the album, although I didn't set out to write that theme.'

131

On a purely musical level even Simon's harshest critics acknowledged the album's strengths. *Graceland* is a glittering, glistening triumph. Commercially the album is a record executive's dream: spanning generations, it is hungrily bought by Simon's fans from the 60s as well as being appreciated by their children who respond instinctively to the strange and infectious rhythms it offers.

From 1st September, 1986 when *Graceland* was released, its pulsing rhythms have poured out of radios, stereos, CDs and cassette players across the world. In the wake of such unexpected success, record companies were keen to exploit the commercial potential of African township music. EMI were quick off the mark in releasing the unrepresentative *Sounds Of Soweto*; while Johnny Clegg also on EMI, (whose own South African investments are not inconsiderable), had his 1987 London show touted as 'The authentic sound of Graceland', whatever that may be!

For too many years, Graceland had symbolized the first lost promise of rock and roll; by the spring of 1987 its name offered the possibility of the dream being reborn. *Graceland* had become synonymous with the rhythms of resistance, it gave the triumphant sound of black South African music a foothold in the market-place of the world and, in doing so, focused attention on the bitter struggle of a nation to reclaim its home.

Rhythms of Resistance

Since its release in the late summer of 1986, *Graceland* has been dogged by controversy. For twenty years Paul Simon had been an established and quietly uncontroversial pop star; with the release of *Graceland* he suddenly found himself pilloried and his motives and actions subjected to a relentless inquisition. Accusations flew thick and fast: critics saw Simon as a quisling who had betrayed the essentially liberal principles of rock and roll, while his champions argued that with *Graceland* he had focused the world's attention on the plight of black South Africa. There were also those, including Simon himself, who were keen to remove the album from the political arena altogether, and viewed it purely in musical terms.

The luxury of remaining above politics is not a real option for any artist with ambitions to be truly relevant, and by choosing to record in South Africa with South African musicians, Paul Simon – whether willingly or not – inevitably placed himself in a political context. The *Graceland* controversy is the most divisive and contentious in the thirty-year history of rock and roll, because it directly confronts the most sensitive political issue of the late twentieth century – the future of South Africa.

By the end of the 1980s, institutionalized racism – or as the South African government euphemistically calls it, 'apartheid' (literally 'separateness') – was approaching its fortieth anniversary. The 1987 (white only) election showed a definite swing to the right, the white minority steadfastly refusing to enter into a ballot box dialogue with the black majority. The BBC's Michael Buerk wrote: 'The election came and went with its unmistakable message: whites want to defend their privileges, whatever the world outside, or the blacks here, may say. It was a mandate for President Botha to crack down harder, rather than push on faster with reform.'

Since the National Party's victory in the 1948 election, the policy of apartheid has systematically become a bulwark of South African life. Prime Minister Verwoerd was the architect of apartheid, and his introduction of the 1950 Acts covering 'Population', 'Group Areas' and 'Immorality' laid the foundation for the racist society which endures today. The rationale for apartheid was based on white supremacy; the Aryan arrogance which took root in the 1950 laws recalled the Nazi ideology which had ended only five years before in a Berlin bunker.

The official opposition to the government's separatist policies, the African National Congress (ANC), was formed in 1912, and banned in 1960. In 1961, exasperated by their inability to hold a peaceful dialogue with the government, the militant Unkhonto we Sizwe (Spear of the Nation) was formed to undertake acts of sabotage against military targets; with its formation came the realization that there could be no reconciliation between black and white in South Africa without bloodshed.

In February 1960, British Prime Minister Harold Macmillan had forecast a 'wind of change . . . blowing through this continent, and whether we like it or not, this growth of national consciousness is a political fact'. Six weeks later, in protest against the insidious Pass Laws, which required all non–whites to carry identification twenty-four hours a day and severely restricted their movements, twenty thousand blacks demonstrated in Sharpeville. By the end of the day sixty-nine protestors had been killed by the government's security forces, and nearly two hundred lay injured. The Sharpeville massacre was a watershed: the brutality of the apartheid regime was now openly on the streets and in the world's headlines. From then on, during the last quarter of a century, South Africa has teetered on the brink of a bloody civil war.

For South Africa, perhaps the most significant event of the 70s took place on 16th June, 1976 when the black township of Soweto exploded. Soweto – an acronym for 'south-western towns' – is the largest black township in South Africa, and during the rebellion, 2,500 young blacks were killed or injured. Soweto became known as 'The Children's Crusade', the initial revolt having been sparked by schoolchildren's refusal to learn Afrikaans – the language of white oppression. The revolt in Soweto was spearheaded by young blacks who had grown up under the appalling apartheid regime and had known nothing else but segregation and hostility, and for whom bad housing, pass laws, and poor medical care and schooling were facts of everyday life. The open insurrection of Soweto was the spearhead for increasing militancy among young blacks.

The continuing arrogance and blinkered stupidity of the bloated white minority remains the unacceptable but official face of South Africa. Today it is a country where sixteen per cent of the population owns eighty-seven per cent of the land, where the amount spent on the education of a black child is only one-sixth of that spent on each white child. It is a country where sexual relations between races are banned, where there is one doctor for every 350 whites but only one for every 90,000 blacks, where four million whites dictate policy to nearly twenty-eight million non-whites.

Any gestures by the white government towards improving the lot of the black majority have been purely cosmetic. The 1959 'Bantu Self-Government Act' laid the foundation for the policy of Bantustans or Homelands, which nominally gave the blacks a home of their own, but which in fact led to mass deportation of urban blacks to infertile stretches of country which they were told to welcome as their 'homeland'.

In response to their intolerable situation, natural leaders emerged within the black majority, the most charismatic of whom was the lawyer Nelson Mandela. In an effort to undermine his authority, the white authorities branded Mandela a communist, but he continued eloquently and patiently to argue his case for a South Africa where black and white could live peacefully together: 'Our fight is against real and not imaginary hardships,' he said in 1962, 'basically we fight against two features which are the hallmarks of African life in South Africa and which are entrenched by legislation which we seek to have repealed. These features are poverty and the lack of human dignity, and we do not need communists or so called "agitators" to teach us about these things.'

In 1964 Mandela was sentenced to life imprisonment, a sentence which, with Mandela aged seventy at the time of writing, the South African government seem determined to enforce literally. From the dock he addressed the court: 'During my lifetime I have dedicated myself to the struggle of the African people. I have fought against white domination and I have fought against black domination. I have cherished the ideal of a democratic and free society in which all persons live together in harmony and with equal opportunities. It is an ideal for which I hope to live and to achieve. But if needs be, it is an ideal for which I am prepared to die.'

Scandalized by the increasingly overt oppression practised by the South African government, the world began belatedly to apply pressure against the racist regime. By 1961 South Africa had been cast out of the Commonwealth, and economic and sporting sanctions had been imposed; but throughout, the white government blithely ignored world protest. Proud of its tenacity, the white minority compared their struggle and isolation with the 'wagons-in-a-circle' laagers of the nineteenth-century Boer farmers who had first colonized the interior. It was the imposition of a cultural boycott by the United Nations in 1980 which first brought the entertainment world into the spotlight of the South African controversy.

The garish public face of the Homelands policy is the entertainment complex, Sun City, a massive pleasure resort set in the heart of Bophuthatswana, where white holidaymakers converge to witness top-line entertainment. The acts from all around the world who appear there are paid fortunes to play before supposedly integrated audiences, but Sun City is a sham. The blacks who pepper the audience are there on complimentary tickets – their wages could never cover the true cost of admission. Many acts who would not otherwise appear in South Africa have played Sun City in the belief that they were performing to truly integrated audiences in an independent Homeland. Those who have appeared at Sun City, often for fees in excess of $1 million, include Ray Charles, Linda Ronstadt, Queen, Rod Stewart, Elton John, Barry Manilow, Cliff Richard, Millie Jackson, Tina Turner, Leo Sayer, George Benson and Frank Sinatra.

The UN's belated reaction to the iniquities of apartheid and the attempted whitewash the government was perpetrating in Sun City came to a head with the 1980 official boycott, which called for 'all States to take steps to prevent all cultural, academic, sporting and other exchanges with South Africa; . . . writers, artists, musicians and other personalities to boycott South Africa, and . . . all academic and cultural institutions to terminate all links with South Africa'.

In Britain the Anti-Apartheid Movement had diligently been picketing sporting events for some time; in tennis, cricket, athletics and rugby, South Africa was slowly becoming isolated from the international sporting scene. Certain British entertainers, however, continued to offer bread and circuses to those privileged South Africans who made the trip to Sun City. John Deacon of Queen, who played eight shows in Sun City in 1984, commented: 'Everybody's been to South Africa, it's not as though we're setting a precedent. Elton John's been there, Cliff Richard, Rod Stewart. I know there can be a bit of a fuss . . . basically, we want to play wherever the fans want to see us.' The group's Brian May stated, 'We're totally against apartheid and all it stands for', but defended their trip by saying, 'We actually met musicians of both colours. They welcomed us with open arms. The only criticism we got was from outside South Africa.' Indeed, a disturbingly large number of rock acts were willing to perform there and take their thirty pieces of silver.

The presence at Sun City of acts such as Queen, Rod Stewart and Linda Ronstadt – who were very much a part of the liberating tradition of rock and roll – was baffling; that successful black acts such as Tina Turner, Millie Jackson and George Benson would play there was incomprehensible. The Beatles always refused to play South Africa, and Gram Parsons quit the Byrds on the eve of a South African tour in 1968 because the group would not be playing to integrated audiences. It is worth recalling that both with Garfunkel and as a solo act, Paul Simon has repeatedly turned down seven-figure sums to perform at Sun City, comparing it with doing a concert in Nazi Germany at the height of the Holocaust.

It took Bruce Springsteen's former guitarist 'Miami' Steve Van Zandt to focus the rock world's attention on the hypocrisies of Sun City. A fact-finding trip to South Africa in 1984 presaged the *Sun City* project of 1985 – a mini album which featured Bob Dylan, Springsteen, Miles Davis, U2's Bono, Lou Reed, Peter Gabriel, Pete Townshend, Bob Geldof, Ringo Starr, Daryl Hall and John Oates. Paul Simon was asked to contribute, but declined because the early demo of the song he was sent accused his friend Linda Ronstadt ('Linda Ronstadt, how could you do that?') Stung by criticisms of his decision not to participate, Simon responded, 'I was offered a million dollars and I turned it down. That was my statement.' In fact, Van Zandt later scrubbed the 'finger-pointing' version of the song on the grounds that he 'didn't want to make value judgements on people who went there. People have gone for all kinds of reasons. The important thing is that they not go back.' The record effectively raised people's consciousness, and among those who agreed never to return to Sun City were Linda Ronstadt, Elton John and Cliff Richard.

By and large, mainstream rock music has ignored the plight of black South Africans. Activists such as Gil Scott-Heron had been on the attack with such songs as 1975's 'Johannesburg', but Peter Gabriel's anthemic 1980 song 'Biko' was the first to fuse white rock with indigenous African rhythms. In the song, Gabriel movingly tackled the death of the black activist Steve Biko in police custody in 1977. The fusion of African and American music continued with Talking Heads' 1980 album *Remain In Light* – incidentally Paul

Simon's favourite Talking Heads album. The rousing Special AKA single 'Nelson Mandela' produced by Elvis Costello in 1984 was a significant contribution, while the promising new band Latin Quarter dedicated 'No Rope As Long As Time' and 'Radio Africa' to the struggle. Stevie Wonder also made an emphatic statement on his 1985 *In Square Circle* album: 'It's Wrong (Apartheid)'.

Jerry Dammers, founder of the Specials (later Special AKA) was in the forefront of Anti Apartheid activity in Britain. Aside from the 'Nelson Mandela' single, he also produced Robert Wyatt and the SWAPO Singers' single, 'Wind Of Change', in 1985; more importantly, he was one of the moving forces behind the formation of Artists Against Apartheid, whose triumphant concert on Clapham Common in the summer of 1986 was one of the largest anti-apartheid protests yet seen in Great Britain. Over a quarter of a million people turned out to protest against the policies of the South African government, and to see and hear music from Elvis Costello, Peter Gabriel, Boy George and dozens more. It was Dammers' close involvement with Artists Against Apartheid that made him one of Simon's most vociferous critics during the *Graceland* tour.

The kernel of the anti-*Graceland* argument is that Paul Simon defiantly flouted the cultural boycott; that by going to record in Johannesburg he offered tacit support to Botha's apartheid policies. His critics further claim that at no time has he specifically condemned apartheid, and that by bringing musicians out of South Africa to perform with him, he has further flouted the boycott.

The first crucial point in any understanding of the situation is that Simon did not violate the cultural boycott as it then stood. The United Nations Anti-Apartheid Committee announced in February 1987 that Simon had not breached the boycott, and that they had therefore 'decided not to place his name on its "Register of Entertainers, Actors and Others Who Have Performed in Apartheid South Africa"'. This followed a letter Simon sent a week before in which he stated that he was 'completely opposed' to apartheid, and that he was working in his field to achieve the end of the system.

To suggest that Paul Simon was a stooge of the South African government and even sympathetic to their apartheid policy is ridiculous. During the 1960s his songs attacked the racist Ku Klux Klan, while his politics were those of a concerned liberal, supporting Democrats McCarthy and McGovern, and trade unionist Cesar Chavez. In a 1969 interview, Simon stated: 'I know where my sympathies lie, they're with the youth movement, Black Power and the New Left.' Speaking of Simon in 1986, his musical colleague Jessy Dixon said: 'He respects blacks and our music. He also respects the culture behind it.'

The problem with a blanket boycott is that it indiscriminately denies a platform in this country to anything that comes out of South Africa, even to the authentic voice of frustrated and oppressed non-whites unable to be heard in their own country. Thus Johnny Clegg – leader of the multi-racial band Savuka and a distinctive strong voice against the iniquities of apartheid – only just managed to slip through the MU ban, although ninety per cent of his music bitterly condemns the South African regime. He told Hugh Fielder of *Sounds* in 1987: 'I just feel it [the cultural boycott] is misinformed and cut off from the reality within South Africa. I believe the boycott is now in a transitional stage. I want it redefined to make it more effective because it's become outdated. . . .'

Simon himself has attacked the 'double boycott' that black South African musicians face; while sympathetic to the idea of isolating the Botha regime in South Africa, he explained his reservations to David Osborne: 'It has had this ironic aspect – it has stopped the culture from coming out. South African artists haven't been heard anywhere in the world because of this double apartheid applied to them. First, they have to live under apartheid, and when they try to export their music, people say "Oh no thank you, that's from South Africa".'

There are those who believe that in order to be truly effective, the boycott must isolate South Africa completely, even if this does lead to the silencing of the very people it sets out to help. The British Musicians Union has doggedly pursued the boycott to the letter. In 1985 they did all they could to ensure that the Soweto group, the Malpoets, were not allowed to perform in London, and only the intervention of the Labour-held Greater London Council enabled the concerts to go ahead. Branches of the Anti-Apartheid Movement have even picketed anti-apartheid plays performed by black theatre groups such as *Bijers Sunbird* and *Poppie Nongena*.

Joe Boyd, who produced *Poppie Nongena* in London in 1985, wrote to *Time Out* at the height of the Graceland controversy, drawing attention to the anachronisms inherent in the dogmatic approach of those who see any breach of the boycott as treachery: 'In all revolutions, nuance and ambivalence are the first casualties. It is hard to put sub-clauses on a banner or explain exceptions in a chanted slogan. I firmly believe it is as important to support the

139

dissemination of the genuine culture of South Africa as it is not to buy Outspan oranges!'

At the press conference in London to launch *Graceland* in August 1986, Simon, when asked about the boycott, said: 'On the one hand I think that the artistic community should make a statement about the moral outrage that they feel; on the other hand, I do think it is beneficial to have cultures exchanging. A free exchange of ideas usually brings people closer together, which makes it easier to have a dialogue, especially the black South African musicians. I think it's a crime that they're not able to come and play around the world. I did check with Harry Belafonte before I left, he had mixed feelings because this time they were dealing with someone who was not going to perform, but to bring back the music. The circumstance was new to them, as it was to the ANC.' At this point the grey areas of the cultural boycott became apparent: Simon was *not* performing before a spuriously 'mixed' audience in Sun City, he was bringing the music and spirit of the black townships out of South Africa, to the world.

Hugh Masekela, who left South Africa in 1960, is convinced that Simon's recording in his homeland and the subsequent tour (featuring exclusively black South African musicians) can only be a force for good, prompting a fuller understanding of the realities of life in South Africa. Masekela's musical and political credentials are impeccable; Nelson Mandela was a regular guest at his concerts in South Africa, while his first trumpet was a gift from Bishop Trevor Huddleston, Chairman of the Anti-Apartheid Movement.

Masekela has known Simon since 1966, and during his quarter of a century in exile has been one of the most outspoken opponents of the regime in South Africa. When we met at the beginning of 1987, he told me he was furious about the criticisms of *Graceland* and Simon's motives: 'There's groups who have played there and taken their millions of dollars, and haven't even left a fucking plectrum. So here's a guy who's going there to try and build something and everyone's going crazy. . . . They should be bugging 10 Downing Street, the White House, the Elysée Palace; that's where the pressure should go. The pressure should go on the businesses propping up this situation. Because really, in the end, when history is written, it won't say that South African people could have been free if Paul Simon hadn't gone and recorded there!'

Prior to joining Simon in London to rehearse for the *Graceland* tour, Masekela took part in a show in Zimbabwe, which documented the history of South African music; he was joined on stage

at the climax of the show by members of the Zimbabwe government and, more significantly, Oliver Tambo, President of the
ANC, who praised the show as a positive message of unity, and
advised Masekela to 'go on and on' displaying the unity of black
South Africa through its music.

'The UN Charter says that people shouldn't perform in South
Africa, it doesn't say anything about recording,' Masekela told me
in London after the Zimbabwe triumph. 'The most successful thing
Paul has done is getting us all together . . . it's a great thing that
someone can go and record South African musicians who are
already under the gun and be able to put them on the international
stage. . . . Rather than helping the South African situation, the
pressure groups are more involved in monitoring it . . . there are
double standards, say some guy in London or New York feels that
it was sinful for Paul to help . . . there's a kind of misdirected energy
in the helping of South Africa. Even our revolution has been
hijacked, because agencies overseas don't feel that they have to
consult with South Africans while they're helping them. Like the
cultural boycott – nobody approached *us*, nobody asked *us*!'

Paul Simon has never been an overtly political writer, although
his best work was set in a disillusioned urban landscape and his
muse wrestled with internal angst, lost ideals, the increasingly
vacuous state of America and its growing disenchantment with its
elected leaders. Simon was too subtle a writer to use *Graceland* as a
soap box from which to shout 'Apartheid Is Wrong!' to an audience
of the converted: 'I assume that people understand that . . .
apartheid is an odious system.' He was, however, always aware of
the implications of what he had done and was willing to confront
the issue. In the aftermath of the album's release, accusations flew
that he had failed to speak out against apartheid; stung by these
criticisms he called a press conference at London's ICA in January
1987, where he tried to explain his thinking: 'Why didn't I come out
and say apartheid is wrong? The audience that I am used to
addressing – I mean this album is a big hit, a Number 1 album,
which hasn't happened to me since the Simon and Garfunkel days –
I don't think I have to talk to beginners. I write to a sophisticated
listening audience, and what I was saying, that the information I
thought was new and interesting, was about the culture. . . . I don't
consider it my responsibility to educate people who have never
heard of apartheid, and for the first time must be told by a pop star
that this is wrong. Pop music is not the forum to discuss complex
political issues . . . I am not a politician. I did not set out to make

a political statement. I was making a cultural statement that has political implications.'

The majority of Simon's critics howled indignantly and seemed immune to the complexities of the situation. One of the few exceptions was Dave Hill in *The Independent*:

'The most worrying aspect of the whole *Graceland* saga rests within the soul of Simon's compositions themselves. The trouble with his rather mannered lyrical introspection . . . is that it betrays an interest in personal angst which is not inherently wrong but the insularity of which, let loose in a South African context can become dangerously inappropriate. . . . Objectively, *Graceland* is a record of considerable creative integrity which has, by its apolitical nature – itself a political stance – become a way into the growing anti-apartheid consensus for people who wish that caring sentiments alone can change the world. They, like Simon, want to touch hands across the ocean but do not concern themselves with who is controlling the swell and what interest they might have in granting you right of passage.'

Even those people who understood Simon's motives and supported his actions were puzzled by his initial naïvety. Peter Gabriel told biographer Spencer Bright in 1987: 'I liked the *Graceland* album but felt that he handled it wrong, and had maybe been a little naïve . . . the musicians he wanted to work with weren't being allowed to leave the country. So the only way he could work with these musicians was to go in there. At that time he asked about the UN ban, he was advised the ban meant live performances as opposed to studio performances. So I think he was quite shaken by the uproar that emerged. He was then advised, when he had finished the recordings, that the ban did apply to studio work. I think he was genuinely innocent of that, but I think he could have had a little more foresight of the possible consequences, and also made a strong declaration earlier on.'

Despite the critics, Simon had plenty of support from those who instinctively understood what he was trying to do, and who saw the whole project as an implicit declaration of where his sympathies lay. Writing in *Azania Frontline*, Roseinnes Phahle underlined this point: 'Critics have said that Simon was naïve to go to South Africa. Perhaps he is naïve, but so too must be Sipho Mabuse and all the leading black South African musicians who have supported Simon; all the progressive newspapers which have reported favourably on Simon and the tour, and most naïve of all must be South Africa's leading musicians Hugh Masekela and Miriam Makeba who for twenty years have sung against apartheid and, as members of Simon's tour, are now supporting Simon with their feet. The President and Prime Minister of Zimbabwe who welcomed the Simon concert to Harare must also be naïve!'

It was undoubtedly the scale of *Graceland*'s success which fanned the flames of the controversy. If the album had been the critical and commercial failure that *Hearts and Bones* was, such a storm would never have been whipped up. The fact that *Graceland* sold in excess of five million copies worldwide – and is still selling – has added an extra dimension of spite to the hostility, for nobody, least of all Simon, anticipated the global success of the album. If he had included a bald anti-apartheid statement on the sleeve, it surely would have been castigated as a meaningless gesture of white liberal guilt; or simply seen as an ageing, has-been pop star's attempt at jumping on the anti-apartheid bandwagon.

At times it seemed as though the persecution of Paul Simon was becoming more important than continuing the struggle against the racist bigotry of South Africa. What seemed to stick in the craw of the music press in particular was that it was Paul Simon of all people who had tapped this rich musical vein. The resentment was manifest, that it was Simon – a forty-five-year-old millionaire whose work, in their revisionist eyes, was tainted by the stain of success – and not one of their own generation who had achieved this fusion.

A further accusation levelled at Simon has been that of cultural imperialism in his attempt to revive a flagging career by riding to new glories on the back of struggling black musicians. This smacks of the false wisdom of hindsight, for Mbaqanga had hardly been prominently featured on radio playlists prior to the release of *Graceland*. Simon called this argument 'intellectually vacant' and told *Hot Press*: '*Graceland* doesn't in any way take away from anybody else's pleasure in South African music. In fact, now let's be honest, most people never heard any South African music before and this idea that the music of one place belongs to that place and shouldn't cross over boundaries is absurd. It's as if you wanted to say to Ray Charles, "Where do you get the nerve to sit there playing that eighteenth-century European instrument?" You know, it's an absurd idea. Music is valid if it's musical. You can't stop music at a border. It's not meant to be. Try music as a universal language.'

Peter Gabriel, whose own knowledge of musical forms is extensive, also recognizes that rock is essentially symbiotic: 'I think

143

there is a lot of bullshit talked about it. Show me an artist who is pure and doesn't feed off other people. Show me a musician who is pure and particularly show me a rock musician who doesn't feed off other people and other styles and other traditions. I think what Paul Simon does is healthy, he has a tradition of doing this. He was the first white musician of any measure of success to take reggae music seriously. Reggae wasn't hip at the time he was working with it. He helped get an interest in South American music and folk music, and that definitely helped musicians trying to get work in Europe and America. And he has definitely increased the stature of South African music with this album.'

Prior to *Graceland*, African music was largely a novelty in pop terms, limited to hits like 'Wimoweh' (aka 'The Lion Sleeps Tonight') and Miriam Makeba's 'Pate Pate' in the 60s, while in the 70s white South African acts such as John Kongos and Clout enjoyed sporadic British chart success. From Nigeria, Osibisa's 'criss-cross rhythms' were briefly in vogue in progressive rock circles. Simon's contemporary, the late Phil Ochs, cut an indigenous single ('Nito Mchum Ba Ngombe') in Kenya in 1973. Nigeria's King Sunny Ade and Fela Kuti provided exciting new sounds in the late 70s and early 80s, but theirs was largely a cult appeal. It took *Graceland* to inject African music into the pop mainstream of the 1980s. The exiled South African trumpeter Hugh Masekela appreciated just how significant a role Simon could play with *Graceland* when he told me: 'European audiences won't go for something unless one of their artists does it. Bossa nova didn't happen before Stan Getz, Eric Clapton did "I Shot the Sheriff" before reggae was taken seriously, Belafonte had a big hit with calypso before he was taken seriously. It always has to start from where the business is, otherwise it doesn't seem to fly. . . . We need more cultural big names for South Africa, they can always get to the media.'

It was not as if African music had remained untainted prior to Simon's involvement; over the years indigenous African music had been diluted by the influence of Western pop, a fact Simon quickly picked up on when he arrived in Johannesburg: 'Every time a musician hears another musician whose music he admires, that influences him. And the South African guys, particularly the players from Soweto, were very influenced by American music long before I got there. When they came over here, they were very influenced by American musicians and recording techniques.'

Paul Simon's *Graceland* not only brought township jive to the world, but helped bring it all back home. Johnny Clegg explained the importance of the album: 'He has done a great service to African music. *Graceland* is actually going black in South Africa now. You hear it everywhere, in taxis, trains and restaurants, and it's turning people back towards their own music. He's given them a new perspective on it.'

Simon was determined that the record should be released in South Africa so that the country which inspired his musical odyssey would be able to hear the fruits of it. With many of their best musicians like Hugh Masekela, Miriam Makeba and Dollar Brand in exile, South Africa was in grave danger of losing its hold on its own music; indigenous acts were moving away from their roots and becoming limp copies of Western acts, covering popular hits and forsaking the authenticity of traditional African music. With the media firmly in the hands of a minority government, with house arrests pinning down the most creative forces within the country, and with their best musicians being denied a world platform, the music of black South Africa was being slowly suffocated. *Graceland* helped in some small way to redress the balance: it became the best selling album in the country since *Thriller* and stood at Number 1 in the South African charts for nine weeks. *Graceland* may well be a significant step towards the people who inspired the album reclaiming their own musical heritage.

Graceland also gave a refreshingly positive image of black South Africans to the world. For too long, all we had seen were the happy, smiling faces of 'integrated' audiences which government propaganda portrayed contrasted with the violence and bloody revenge which was reported everywhere before the 1985 State of Emergency clamped down on the free flow of information. Joseph Shabalala has spoken of music being 'only a force for good. It's a force for joy and understanding.' Certainly, through the music of *Graceland*, Paul Simon has given a face to a faceless majority and has helped bring the music of the Third World to the privileged First World.

'The major problem with the critics of Paul Simon', Roseinnes Phahle has suggested, 'is that they are confusing apartheid South Africa with the black people of South Africa, their art, music and culture.' Simon has shown the very positive side of that culture; the world now knows that there is more to South Africa than violence, hatred and bloodshed. We have now all felt the boundless potential of a stifled nation still fighting for life after years of needless suffering, but with the spirit and strength to continue until freedom is won.

Paul Simon has resigned himself to the likelihood that the *Graceland* issue will dog him for the rest of his career; but his efforts have helped to bring the situation in South Africa to the attention of millions whose knowledge of the true face of apartheid was blinkered. As the epicentre of the whirlwind, Simon reflected in the summer of 1986: 'People tend to look at all aspects of South African life through the prism of politics, but really this was primarily about music. That was a hard thing to explain sometimes. Not to deny the political implications, but they were implications. For me, music is a universal language through which we all connect. Art has a moral position inevitably, and showing the life of the country through its music makes it easier to understand the humanity of the situation. I mean, I don't know *anybody* who is pro apartheid except for Afrikaaners. I have a tremendous fear of a civil war type bloodbath there, on a personal level now, because I know people, black and white, their children. So I guess this album is meant to be a very small statement, an introduction to people we only knew through newsreels; now we'll know them on a more personal level.'

In the acrimony which followed the album's release, what was frequently overlooked was the quality of the music; the real, permanent triumph of *Graceland* is that it brought to the world a rich strand of music which had previously gone unheard outside Africa. Fired by the musical impetus, Simon now prepared to take *Graceland* on the road; he was determined that the tour should broaden the perspective of the album and that the rhythms of resistance should ring out loud and clear. 'The album is not political in the sense of rhetoric. But it certainly is political in the sense that I'm working with black South African artists and I'm working with a form of music that's indigenous to South Africa. But the tour . . . will be the music of South Africa and will be a strong anti–apartheid statement in itself.'

All Around the World

On 1st February, 1987, five months to the day since the release of *Graceland*, Paul Simon walked on stage in Rotterdam to launch the most controversial rock tour of the 1980s. His tiny figure stood briefly centre stage and welcomed the audience to 'an evening of music from South Africa'.

Political problems aside, the logistics of mounting a tour of the size and complexity of *Graceland* were enormous. Simon has never been enthusiastic about touring, and the *Graceland* concerts were fraught with more than the usual difficulties. To begin with, the likelihood of getting the performers from the album onto concert stages outside South Africa seemed remote; financially too, the expense of mounting a worldwide tour with such a large troupe of musicians was prohibitive. However, with the staggering success of the album providing funds, and with Simon's dogged determination to bring the township music out of the ghetto, the tour went ahead.

Hugh Masekela, whose prior commitments had stopped him appearing on *Graceland*, was delighted to be given the opportunity to tour with Simon. The trumpeter in turn suggested that his ex-wife Miriam Makeba be invited along as a special guest. For many years Miriam Makeba – 'Mama Africa' – had been the proud voice of black Africa in exile. Her testimony to the United Nations in 1963 had alerted the world to the iniquities inside South Africa, and during her long exile she had sung across the world songs of freedom: a lone voice defiant against the broadside of Pretoria.

It was now two years since the album had been recorded and many of the contributors were unavailable for the concerts; using London as a base, Simon gathered a hand-picked team of black African musicians and began rehearsals for the tour. To feature Rockin' Dopsie and Los Lobos in addition to the cast of twenty-four African musicians proved impossible, and consequently the

147

Dopsie and Lobos songs from *Graceland* were the only tracks not featured in concert.

Spiritually uplifting, ideologically sound and musically mesmerizing, the *Graceland* concerts during the first half of 1987 were inspiring on every level. From the opening instrumental, 'Township Jive', through to the jubilant conclusion of 'N'Kosi Sikeleli' – the ANC anthem – the shows were a triumph. Simon himself was a shadowy figure; almost a guest at his own concert, he remained in the background while his friends performed to delighted, capacity crowds around the world.

'The Boy In The Bubble' was the first song from the album to be performed in concert, heralded by Tony Cedras' accordion. The songs from *Graceland* were brilliantly recreated on stage, the passionate ensemble playing enriching the material with purpose and delight. Even the weakest tracks from the album such as 'Gumboots' and 'I Know What I Know' came alive, particularly 'Gumboots', which segued into a joyous cover of the Del-Vikings' 1957 hit 'Whispering Bells' and gave backing singers Sonti Mndebele, Nomsa Calusa and Nobambo Fazerkerley a chance to shine. It was a perfect moment of unity which spanned thirty years of rock history from an almost forgotten relic of the 50s through to a track from the most important album of the 80s, and singing it was Paul Simon, the man for whom it all came together as one.

Live, 'You Can Call Me Al' was driven on steam with the brass interjections packing an almost undreamed of punch. The only pre-*Graceland* Simon originals were 'The Boxer' and an Africanized 'Mother and Child Reunion' which in this context achieved a sublime majesty – Simon's reflection on life and death taking on a whole new layer of meaning. 'The Boxer', bloody but unbowed, symbolized in this context a whole nation of fighters; and as Simon sang the lines '*Still, a man hears what he wants to hear/And disregards the rest*' he must have been thinking of the dogmatists who had closed their hearts and minds to his vision.

Hugh Masekela's set was equally impressive, notably his plea for the release of Nelson Mandela, 'Bring Him Back Home', and for the sight of him standing with fist clenched defiantly in the air during the ANC anthem while the impassioned voices on stage sang '*God bless Africa, raise up our descendants, hear our prayers*'. Miriam Makeba's heartfelt interpretation of Masekela's 'Soweto Blues' registered strongly, as did her speech: 'I'm looking forward to the day when we will have the opportunity to invite Paul Simon to perform with us in a free South Africa!' It seemed incomprehensible that outside the doors of the Royal Albert Hall pickets were protesting at Simon's alleged support of the white government in South Africa, while inside, on stage, an intensely moving and spirited anti-apartheid show was taking place.

Universally, unquestionably and obviously to Simon's delight, the stars of the show were Ladysmith Black Mambazo. Hearing them on record was, God knows, impressive enough; but to see them soar and swoop in perfect unison of voice and movement was a sight few will ever forget. Ladysmith Black Mambazo sparkled with 'Diamonds On The Soles Of Her Shoes', while 'Homeless' was almost unbearably moving. Joseph Shabalala's spirituality was perhaps most apparent during the poignant blending of his own 'King Of Kings' with 'Amazing Grace'. The awesome scope of Ladysmith's ten voices was accompanied by 'cothoza mfana' – the act of bouncing quickly and lightly on your toes.

While in London Joseph told me: 'I used to tell Paul "your voice is very nice, you have a good voice, your voice can touch somebody" . . . I think this guy has a gift from God.' The look on Simon's face as Joseph led Black Mambazo through their intricate vocal and dance routine on stage broadcast his belief that Joseph's gifts came from somewhere special too, and that the luck was his in having the opportunity to work with Ladysmith.

For its participants, the highlight of the tour came in mid-February, after barely a fortnight on the road, when the ensemble played two shows at Harare's Rutfaro Stadium in Zimbabwe, the closest frontline state to South Africa and the nearest the exiled musicians can ever get to home. Zimbabwe's much acclaimed Bhundu Boys – now labelmates of Simon's – were disparaging about his motives, but Prime Minister Robert Mugabe proved very supportive. Over 40,000 delighted fans, many of whom had travelled up from South Africa, packed the stadium for the largest multi-racial gathering in the country's eight-year history. As the thousands of voices swelled together for the ANC anthem in the warm African night, the message carried on the wind toward the South. Simon, the architect, could not help but feel humbled by what he had begun: 'This is an experience I will never forget. This is a homecoming for most of the singers and the band, we've come to a frontline state – as close as we are allowed to be to South Africa. It's a wonderful experience.'

The interplay between artists and audience was tangible; politically, musically, emotionally, this was the culmination. Ray Phiri, leader of the band Stimela, who had worked closely alongside

Simon during the album and tour, talked to *Rolling Stone* about the Harare show: 'It was the biggest high of my life. But I knew my people would love it. . . . It was this Jewish man from New York who made it happen for us. Now the world knows about South African music. People out here who feel the emotion in our music know that we are going through trying times. Our music gives people hope.' It was only fitting that the official video of the tour, *Graceland – The African Concert*, should have been filmed at Harare.

The unity apparent in Harare was marred in London by the presence outside the Royal Albert Hall of pickets from the Anti-Apartheid Movement and Artists Against Apartheid. The pickets were distributing leaflets to concert-goers which read in part, 'The UN cultural boycott is about not going to South Africa to perform, record or promote records: a policy Paul Simon says he supports. Then let him say he will not return to South Africa until apartheid is dismantled. That is what the UN has asked of him. But Paul Simon hasn't given that commitment: he seems to think he's above politics. But he can't ignore politics when South Africans die daily in political struggle for basic human rights. . . . Think long and hard before you go to Paul Simon's concerts or listen to *Gracelands* [*sic*]. You might like the music, but there are more important issues.'

Members of AAA also handed in a letter addressed to Paul Simon at the Royal Albert Hall on 7th April, 1987, the opening night of Simon's six-night run at the venue. Signed, among others, by Jerry Dammers, Billy Bragg and Paul Weller, it demanded that Simon give 'a complete and heartfelt public apology to the UN General Assembly for breaching the cultural, academic and other boycotts . . .'

In fact, Simon had not breached the cultural boycott in the first place. The UN's ban at the time of his trip to Johannesburg was concerned specifically with live performances. When the reproaches began, Simon wrote to the UN to clarify his position; his letter of 29th January, 1987 concluded: 'As an artist who has refused to perform in South Africa I reiterate and intend to maintain this position in the context of the UN cultural boycott.' The UN were obviously satisfied by Simon's reassurances, and less than a week later announced that his name would not be placed on their blacklist.

Exactly two years after Simon recorded in South Africa, the UN did decide however to extend the parameters of the cultural boycott to include other 'culturally-related activity involving South Africa including: performing, recording, participating in the making of a film, attending a cultural event, and supporting or otherwise assisting in the organising or carrying-out of any other cultural activity there'.

The debate prompted by *Graceland* highlighted schisms within the protest movement: the split between those who were in favour of a total boycott to isolate South Africa completely from the rest of the world, and those who felt that dissenting voices from within South Africa should be given a platform in the outside world became apparent. A total boycott would obviously preclude Simon's *Graceland*, but also Ladysmith Black Mambazo's twenty-five albums and those of Johnny Clegg or Sipho Mabuse; anything, in fact – however critical of the Botha regime – which emanated from South Africa.

Opponents of a total boycott, while understanding the need to stifle government propaganda disguised as 'culture', feel that black indigenous artists have a vital role to play in keeping the world's attention focused on the problems of South Africa. They would argue that to undermine a government you have to take away its bedrock of financial support. A government as firmly entrenched as Botha's will never be culturally starved out of power; financial withdrawal, however, is crucial. It is the billions of pounds that outside governments allow to be pumped into South Africa which prop up apartheid – not Paul Simon's hotel bills.

During the furore surrounding *Graceland* and the concerts, those who were quick off the mark to criticize Simon often allowed their dogmatism to obscure the real issues, and there was evidence of double standards being applied. Simon's seventeen-day working stay was cited as bolstering the Botha regime, although Malcolm McLaren's trip to record parts of his 1983 *Duck Rock* album in Soweto and Steve Van Zandt's fact-finding visits in 1984 had largely escaped criticism.

Rolling Stone pointed out that with *Graceland* Simon had 're-minded us that art is in itself political – much to the consternation of the windy politicos who thought they owned the franchise on racial harmonizing'. The fact that the 'windy politicos' included one of the British rock scene's most honourable musicians is a sad truth. For all his criticisms of Simon – and at times it did seem like he was conducting a witch-hunt – Jerry Dammers' contribution to music in the 80s cannot be overstated, as he virtually single-handedly proved that engaging pop music could be married to politically relevant and provocative lyrics.

By and large the international community of musicians were firmly behind Simon. Elvis Costello, who produced Dammers'

151

'Nelson Mandela' single and had played at the AAA concert on Clapham Common, attended one of the *Graceland* shows in London, as did Phil Collins, Annie Lennox, Dream Academy, Bob Geldof, Christine McVie and Mick Fleetwood; while at the Los Angeles show Michael Jackson thrilled to the sight and sounds of Ladysmith Black Mambazo.

Peter Gabriel, also prominent in the anti-apartheid fight, spoke out against a complete boycott: 'I think *Graceland* has done an enormous amount for South African music. What really pisses me off about the bans are that I support the prevention of rich white musicians, or Westerners, going to South Africa and taking a lot of money out and supporting the government in that way. However, there are many black artists, writers, painters, musicians, that need to get heard, and that are really talking about their experience in that country at this time. The Musicians Union ban and the Equity ban can forbid their voice being heard. And that must be counter-productive.'

Los Lobos drummer Luis Perez commented: 'I think that what he did wasn't a violation of black South African musicians, he wasn't exploiting them, he was supporting their culture, bringing it to a wider audience. I think he did justice to their culture.' Irish chanteuse Mary Coughlan told Ken Hunt: 'I think that album's incredible. . . . I think what he's done for black South African musicians is incredible, by going there and doing the album, by using their musicians.' While veteran bluesman Taj Mahal also felt that, 'if the album brought people together it's a good thing'. Senegalese musician Youssou N'Dour, who appeared on *Graceland* and has worked with Peter Gabriel, approved of Simon's odyssey and saw *Graceland* as 'a marker for what *could* happen in the future'.

One person who has been strangely silent since the *Graceland* volcano erupted is Harry Belafonte, a member of the New York Anti-Apartheid Co-ordinating Council, who acted as go-between for Simon and the ANC and condoned Simon's trip to Johannesburg; nothing has been heard, either, from Quincy Jones, another friend who originally believed that Simon's visit could do only good. Belafonte and Simon still appear to be working together for the common cause, however. They jointly produced the vehemently anti-apartheid play *Asinamali* which opened off Broadway on the day of Simon's last London show. Simon invested around £200,000 in the all-black production. Simon has also donated the proceeds of the second American leg of the *Graceland* tour to children's charities – including one devoted to children imprisoned in South Africa; Amnesty International estimate that over 7,000 children are in detention there, 2,000 of whom are under sixteen.

As the official voice of black South Africa, it is a shame that the ANC has failed publicly to support Simon's actions or to see the *Graceland* shows as a positive contribution to the anti-apartheid struggle. Indeed, the name of the ANC has been repeatedly invoked by the anti-Simon lobby, largely on the basis of a telegram widely but selectively quoted. The telegram from ANC Headquarters in Lusaka to their office in Sweden was not released to the press, but the part which has surfaced reads: 'The ANC fully support a boycott action against a Paul Simon European and American tour. . . . He has singularly done more harm in flouting the cultural boycott against the racist regime.'

Azania Frontline (the newsletter of the Azania [South Africa] Liberation Support Committee) carried a feature in their March 1987 issue by Roseinnes Phahle, who was also baffled by the absence of official comment from the ANC: 'Though the name and authority of the ANC is used freely by the critics of Paul Simon, the ANC itself has not uttered a word on the Paul Simon visit to South Africa and his recording of part of *Graceland* there. . . . Policy statements are usually issued in the name of the Executive Committee or through the President or General Secretary of the ANC. All have remained silent. . . . But the critics have claimed a telex sent by ANC head office in Lusaka to ANC office in Sweden supported a boycott of Paul Simon . . . however, these claims are no substitute for an official statement from the organization itself or the President himself.'

Having failed to find any official statement from the ANC hierarchy, I repeatedly approached the ANC office in London both by phone and letter but received no response. There was however an indication that the ANC's attitude towards the boycott issue was being reconsidered in the light of *Graceland*. Tom Sebina, the ANC's Information Officer in Lusaka, told *New Musical Express* in April, 1987: 'It is a matter we have been discussing, especially since the development with Paul Simon and the crowd that surround him. We are discussing the situation regarding musicians and other entertainers coming out of South Africa and performing elsewhere in the world and whether it is wise for them to do so.'

The outcome of these deliberations was spelt out in detail by ANC President Oliver Tambo when at the end of May, 1987 he delivered the Canon Collins Memorial Lecture in London. Speaking of the academic and cultural boycotts, he said: 'We must take into account the changes that have taken place over time. In particular, as in almost every other field of human endeavour in South Africa, there has emerged a definable alternative democratic culture – the people's culture permeated with and giving expression to the deepest aspirations of our people in struggle, immersed in democratic and enduring human values. . . . The change that has occurred is that this people's culture, despite the extreme hostility of the racist state, has grown into a mighty stream, distinct from and in opposition to the warped and moribund culture of racism. Its foremost exponents are today part of the democratic movement . . . without doubt the developing and vibrant culture of our people in struggle and its structures need to be supported, strengthened and enhanced. . . . Not only should these not be boycotted, but more, they should be supported, encouraged and treated as the democratic counterparts within South Africa of similar institutions and organizations internationally.'

The man who sparked off the whole controversy was saying much the same thing; as the *Graceland* tour wound down Paul Simon told *Billboard*: 'What I'm facing is the Goebbels philosophy, that if you keep repeating a lie often enough, a certain percentage of people are going to believe it. . . . Essentially, I am doing what the South African government has said is illegal: working with black musicians, sharing royalties and sharing a musical experience. The thing about culture is that it flows, like water. It is impossible for cultures to survive in isolation. The terrible danger about the boycott is that it is imposing a double prejudice against the very people whom it's meant to help. I believe the point's been missed entirely.'

The phenomenon that was *Graceland* swept polls across the world during the early part of 1987. It won Simon his third Grammy, an achievement equalled only by Frank Sinatra and Stevie Wonder. The album also won Simon the equivalent British music industry award: the BPI Best International Album. The public, too, overwhelmingly voted it Album of the Year in publications across the world including *The London Evening Standard*, Ireland's *Hot Press* and America's *Rolling Stone*. The latter's Critics' Poll also acclaimed Simon as 'Best Songwriter' and 'Comeback of the Year'. Contemporary impact aside, *Graceland* is now enshrined in the rock and roll Hall of Fame as one of the most important albums of all time. Paul Simon appears twice in *Rolling Stone*'s list of the hundred best albums since *Sgt. Pepper*, with *Bridge Over Troubled Water*, and *Graceland* registered at Number 56. The list contains only twelve titles from the 80s and of these *Graceland* is the most recent, being the only record from the last three years to be chosen.

Having successfully escaped once from the shadow of his past with Simon and Garfunkel, *Graceland*, nearly two decades later, has given Simon a creative rebirth which none of his contemporaries has equalled, and has led to the re-release of his first five solo albums – including the pre-Simon and Garfunkel album, *The Paul Simon Songbook*, which had been unavailable for many years. What must concern Paul Simon now is how he can keep pace with himself.

As the album itself recedes into history, Simon is still involved with the people he met and formed friendships with during *Graceland*; as well as producing Ladysmith Black Mambazo's *Shaka Zulu* in 1987, an album by Ray Phiri's band Stimela, also produced by Simon, is set for release in 1988. At the end of the *Graceland* tour Paul Simon contemplated his future: 'I don't want to stop because of the momentum of *Graceland*. This is a mistake I've made in the past. I do something good and the natural inclination is to continue. . . . Whatever happens, I'm sure there will be elements of this experience that I will take with me to the next piece of work, though I don't know yet what they are. I like playing with these musicians. They are a great, great band – as good as any I've had. We're friends now. I expect to know these people for life.'

But of the man himself, what information pertains? He is a slight man, edging towards fifty, though you'd never guess it from the cherubic face and full head of hair; a millionaire before he was thirty, a proud and devoted father, a determined and pedantic man; prodigiously talented but far from prolific – his canon over thirty years amounts to little over a hundred songs. The public face of Paul Simon presents a sensitive, questing soul. A restless man, Simon has proved adept at covering his tracks; like a rattlesnake he has shed his skin when necessary. His friends are drawn from an elite, artistic coterie, are largely affluent, east coast intellectuals. He is a man blessed with three bites at the apple, but drawing little comfort from his success; wary of the acclaim that fame and fortune have brought him.

He divides his time between his New York apartment, his Long Island home and the Brill Building office which is full of memorabilia of his two abiding passions – rock and roll and baseball. A native New Yorker, he is known anywhere on the planet that has a hit parade. Unable and unwilling to rely on a past which could assure him an easy future, though in the fortunate position of being financially secure, with no money worries for himself or his family,

155

he is driven towards recognition and acclaim from 'a jury of his peers'. No rolling stone, not haunted by hellhounds on his trail, not driven by demons, but more a songwriter in the tradition of an earlier age – rich, observant, caustic and, above all, a scrupulous craftsman.

As with many creative artists, there is a dichotomy inherent in Paul Simon: here is a man who burst into tears when Richard Nixon was elected in 1968, yet did not feel moved at all by Ronald Reagan's landslide in 1980; a man who can donate $1.5 million to charity at the end of the *Graceland* tour, and yet has a reputation for being arrogant and ungenerous; a man hailed as one of the few genuine poets rock music has produced – a citation abetted by album sales nudging fifty million – but whose own 'Rosebud' is the memory of a baseball game from thirty years before. Timothy White, in his excellent *Crawdaddy* piece of the mid-70s, wrote of Simon's 'quietly compelling combination of something both childlike and fatefully visionary'.

Simon conquered the dreaded writer's block and managed to eschew the creative stimuli of drink and drugs. In the mid-70s, at the very moment when he could have rested comfortably on his laurels and looked back with satisfaction on his career, Simon undertook songwriting tuition and later sought psychiatric advice in the period leading up to *Hearts and Bones*. Such moves indicate that, for all his prodigious talent, Simon is nagged by a degree of self-doubt which no external praise can lessen.

Graceland marked the beginning of a new phase in Simon's career, but as always one with roots in his musical past. What sent Simon to South Africa was the same impetus that had fired him thirty years before to travel uptown to Times Square, and that in his mid-twenties slipped him across the Atlantic to Europe where he created a body of work which still resonates today.

Black African music was one of the strands which Elvis Presley wove into rock and roll in Memphis' Sun Studios in 1954; but Paul Simon went back even further and introduced the world to the music in a purer and more recognizable form. It was Thomas Wolfe who wrote 'You can never go home again'; but everyone tries and with *Graceland* Paul Simon came back to where it all began.

Hairstyles and attitudes may change, but Paul Simon is still driven by the same thing, which bodes well for more of the magical music which has filled his life so far. Late in life he has had '*a shot at redemption*'; as the 80s draw to a close it will be fascinating to see how he uses it.

Discography

Paul Simon solo albums:

The Paul Simon Songbook★ (CBS, 1965):
    I Am A Rock
    Leaves That Are Green
    A Church Is Burning
    April Come She Will
    The Sound Of Silence
    A Most Peculiar Man
    He Was My Brother
    Kathy's Song
    The Side Of A Hill
    A Simple Desultory Philippic
    Flowers Never Bend With The Rainfall
    Patterns

Paul Simon★ (CBS, 1972):
    Mother and Child Reunion
    Duncan
    Everything Put Together Falls Apart
    Run That Body Down
    Armistice Day
    Me and Julio Down By The Schoolyard
    Peace Like A River
    Papa Hobo
    Hobo's Blues
    Paranoia Blues
    Congratulations

There Goes Rhymin' Simon★ (CBS, 1973):
    Kodachrome
    Tenderness

Take Me To The Mardi Gras
Something So Right
One Man's Ceiling Is Another Man's Floor
American Tune
Was A Sunny Day
Learn How To Fall
Saint Judy's Comet
Loves Me Like A Rock

Live Rhymin'★ (CBS, 1974):
Me and Julio Down By The Schoolyard
Homeward Bound
American Tune
El Condor Pasa
Duncan
The Boxer
Mother and Child Reunion
The Sound Of Silence
Jesus Is The Answer (Jessy Dixon Singers)
Bridge Over Troubled Water
Loves Me Like A Rock
America

Still Crazy After All These Years★ (CBS, 1975):
Still Crazy After All These Years
My Little Town
I Do It For Your Love
50 Ways To Leave Your Lover
Night Game
Gone At Last
Some Folks' Lives Roll Easy
Have A Good Time
You're Right
Silent Eyes

Greatest Hits, Etc. (CBS, 1977):
Slip Slidin' Away
Stranded In A Limousine
Still Crazy After All These Years
Have A Good Time
Duncan
Me and Julio Down By The Schoolyard

Something So Right
Kodachrome
I Do It For Your Love
50 Ways To Leave Your Lover
American Tune
Mother and Child Reunion
Loves Me Like A Rock
Take Me To The Mardi Gras

One Trick Pony (Warner Bros, 1980):
Late In The Evening
That's Why God Made The Movies
One Trick Pony
How The Heart Approaches What It Yearns
Oh, Marion
Ace In The Hole
Nobody
Jonah
God Bless The Absentee
Long, Long Day

Hearts and Bones (Warner Bros, 1983):
Allergies
Hearts and Bones
When Numbers Get Serious
Think Too Much (b)
Song About The Moon
Think Too Much (a)
Train In The Distance
René And Georgette Magritte With Their Dog After The War
Cars Are Cars
The Late Great Johnny Ace

Graceland (Warner Bros, 1986):
The Boy In The Bubble
Graceland
I Know What I Know
Gumboots
Diamonds On The Soles Of Her Shoes
You Can Call Me Al
Under African Skies
Homeless

Crazy Love Vol. II
That Was Your Mother
All Around The World Or The Myth Of Fingerprints

(★ The albums marked thus were reissued on Warner Bros in October 1987)

Simon and Garfunkel albums:

Wednesday Morning 3 A.M. (CBS 1964, [UK 1968]):
    You Can Tell The World
    Last Night I Had The Strangest Dream
    Bleecker Street
    Sparrow
    Benedictus
    The Sounds Of Silence
    He Was My Brother
    Peggy-O
    Go Tell It On The Mountain
    The Sun Is Burning
    The Times They Are A-Changin'
    Wednesday Morning 3 A.M.

The Sounds Of Silence (CBS, 1966):
    The Sounds Of Silence
    Leaves That Are Green
    Blessed
    Kathy's Song
    Somewhere They Can't Find Me
    Anji
    Homeward Bound
    Richard Cory
    A Most Peculiar Man
    April Come She Will
    We've Got A Groovey Thing Goin'
    I Am A Rock

(NB: 'Homeward Bound' didn't appear on the American edition of this album)

Parsley, Sage, Rosemary and Thyme (CBS, 1966):
    Scarborough Fair/Canticle
    Patterns

Cloudy
The Big Bright Green Pleasure Machine
The 59th Street Bridge Song (Feelin' Groovy)
The Dangling Conversation
Flowers Never Bend With The Rainfall
A Simple Desultory Philippic (Or How
    I Was Robert McNamara'd Into Submission)
For Emily, Whenever I May Find Her
A Poem On The Underground Wall
7 O'Clock News/Silent Night

(NB: 'Homeward Bound' appears on the US edition of this album)

Simon and Garfunkel (Allegro, 1967):
    Hey Schoolgirl
    Our Song
    That's My Story
    Teenage Fool
    Tia-juana Blues
    Dancin' Wild
    Don't Say Goodbye
    Two Teenagers
    True Or False
    Simon Says

(NB: Collection of Tom and Jerry singles, only released to cash in
on Simon and Garfunkel's current success, and soon deleted)

The Graduate (CBS, 1968):
    The Sounds Of Silence
    The Singleman's Party Foxtrot★
    Mrs Robinson (instrumental)
    Sunporch Cha-Cha★
    Scarborough Fair/Canticle
    On The Strip★
    April Come She Will
    The Folks★
    The Great Effect★
    The Big Bright Green Pleasure Machine
    Whew★
    Mrs Robinson
    The Sounds Of Silence

(★ indicates Dave Grusin's incidental music)

Bookends (CBS, 1968):
    Bookends Theme
    Save The Life Of My Child
    America
    Overs
    Voices Of Old People
    Old Friends
    Bookends Theme
    Fakin' It
    Punky's Dilemma
    Mrs Robinson
    A Hazy Shade Of Winter
    At The Zoo

Bridge Over Troubled Water (CBS, 1970):
    Bridge Over Troubled Water
    El Condor Pasa
    Cecilia
    Keep The Customer Satisfied
    So Long, Frank Lloyd Wright
    The Boxer
    Baby Driver
    The Only Living Boy In New York
    Why Don't You Write Me
    Bye Bye Love
    Song For The Asking

Simon and Garfunkel's Greatest Hits (CBS, 1972):
    Mrs Robinson
    For Emily, Whenever I May Find Her
    The Boxer
    The 59th Street Bridge Song (Feelin' Groovy)
    The Sound Of Silence
    I Am A Rock
    Scarborough Fair/Canticle
    Homeward Bound
    Bridge Over Troubled Water
    America
    Kathy's Song
    El Condor Pasa
    Bookends
    Cecilia

The Simon and Garfunkel Collection (CBS, 1981):
    I Am A Rock
    Homeward Bound
    America
    59th Street Bridge Song
    Wednesday Morning 3 A.M.
    El Condor Pasa
    At The Zoo
    Scarborough Fair/Canticle
    The Boxer
    Sound Of Silence
    Mrs Robinson
    Keep The Customer Satisfied
    Song For The Asking
    Hazy Shade Of Winter
    Cecilia
    Old Friends/Bookends Theme
    Bridge Over Troubled Water

The Concert In Central Park (Geffen, 1982):
    Mrs Robinson
    Homeward Bound
    America
    Me and Julio Down By The Schoolyard
    Scarborough Fair
    April Come She Will
    Wake Up Little Susie
    Still Crazy After All These Years
    American Tune
    Late In The Evening
    Slip Slidin' Away
    A Heart In New York
    Kodachrome/Maybelline
    Bridge Over Troubled Water
    Fifty Ways To Leave Your Lover
    The Boxer
    Old Friends
    The 59th Street Bridge Song (Feelin' Groovy)
    The Sounds Of Silence

Bibliography

The Billboard Book of USA Top 40 Hits, Joel Whitburn (Guinness, 1985)

Bringing It All Back Home, Robbie Woliver (Pantheon, 1987)

Clive: Inside the Record Business, Clive Davis (William Morrow, 1973)

The Electric Muse: The Story of Folk Into Rock, Dave Laing, Karl Dallas, Robin Denselow, Robert Shelton (Methuen, 1975)

The Glory and the Dream: A Narrative History Of America 1932–1972, William Manchester (Michael Joseph, 1975)

The Guinness Book of British Hit Singles (5th edition), Jo and Tim Rice, Mike Read, Paul Gambaccini (Guinness, 1985)

The Illustrated NME Encyclopedia of Rock, ed. Nick Logan and Bob Woffinden (Salamander, 1977)

One Trick Pony, Paul Simon (Alfred A. Knopf, 1980)

Paul Simon: Now and Then, Spencer Leigh (Raven, 1973)

Papa John: The Autobiography of John Phillips (Virgin, 1987)

Simon and Garfunkel, Mitchell S. Cohen (Sire, 1977)

Simon and Garfunkel, John Swenson (W. H. Allen, 1984)

South Africa, Background to the Crisis, Michael Atwell (Sidgwick & Jackson, 1986)

Sun City, The Making of the Record, Dave Marsh (Penguin, 1985)

Written In My Soul, Bill Flanagan (Contemporary, 1987)